AF324016

Regional Disparities, Smaller States
and Statehood for Telangana

About the Author

C.H. Hanumantha Rao, formerly Chairman, Institute of Economic Growth (IEG) Delhi and Centre for Economic and Social Studies (CESS) Hyderabad is presently Hony. Professor at the above institutions. He was a Fellow at the Institute of Economic Growth, University of Delhi (1961-1992) and also its Director (1976-1980).

In addition to a distinguished academic career, Professor Rao has been at the forefront of several high-level policy-making bodies under Government of India. He was a Member, Planning Commission; Seventh and Eighth Finance Commissions; Economic Advisory Council to the Prime Minister; Board of Directors, Reserve Bank of India; National Advisory Council; and Chairman, National Commission on Rural Labour; High Powered Fertilisers Pricing Policy Review Committee.

His publications include *Technological Change and Distribution of Gains in Indian Agriculture* (Macmillan, 1975); *Agricultural Growth, Rural Poverty and Environment Degradation in India* (OUP, 1994); *Andhra Pradesh Development: Economic Reforms and Challenges Ahead* (edited with S. Mahendra Dev, CESS, 2003); *Essays on Agricultural Growth, Farm Size and Rural Poverty Alleviation in India* (AF, 2005); *Agriculture, Food Security, Poverty, and Environment* (OUP, 2005); and *Essays on Development Strategy, Regional Disparities and Centre-State Financial Relations in India* (AF, 2005) and over 100 research papers in academic journals.

Professor Rao has received many awards during his illustrious career including the prestigious 'Padma Bhushan' by the President of India in 2004.

Regional Disparities, Smaller States and Statehood for Telangana

C.H. Hanumantha Rao

ACADEMIC FOUNDATION

NEW DELHI

www.academicfoundation.com

First published in 2010
by

ACADEMIC FOUNDATION
4772-73 / 23 Bharat Ram Road, (23 Ansari Road),
Darya Ganj, New Delhi - 110 002 (India).
Phones : 23245001 / 02 / 03 / 04.
Fax : +91-11-23245005.
E-mail : books@academicfoundation.com
www. academicfoundation.com

Regional Disparities, Smaller States and Statehood for Telangana
by C.H. Hanumantha Rao

ISBN 13: 9788171888269
ISBN 10: 8171888267

Typeset by Italics India, New Delhi.
Printed and bound in India.

Contents

List of Tables
and Appendices

Tables

Appendices

Introduction

Reducing regional disparities in development has been a major concern throughout the plan period. These disparities were largely inherited from the pre-Independence period partly because of the regional diversity in natural endowments and also because of the differences in land tenure systems, investment patterns and systems of governance in different parts of the country which were basically designed to serve the interests of the colonial government and of a large number of princely states.

Reform of land tenures and the development of infrastructure in the backward regions received a high priority in the post-Independence period. Programmes for the development of drought-prone areas, hill and tribal areas were launched from time to time. Federal financial transfers through the successive Finance Commissions and the Planning Commission have distinctly favoured the less developed states over a period of time. Yet, there are limits to such transfers in a democratic polity, especially because many of the so-called richer states are also poor in absolute terms. Thus, inter-state disparities in the levels of development persisted and even increased in some cases. Clearly, apart from the differences in infrastructure and institutions inherited from the pre-Independence period, these disparities are explained by the failure to bridge the gaps in the post-Independence period.

For the same reasons, the disparities in development between different regions within certain larger states persisted. They even increased in certain cases, especially where the backward regions do not have the necessary political clout in decision-making regarding public investment and provision of jobs. This led to regional tensions and persistent demands for carving out separate states consisting of such backward areas. A number of such states have already been constituted. Uttarakhand, Jharkhand and Chhattisgarh are some recent examples.

There has been a marked increase in inter-state disparities in development in the post-reform period. In general, the relatively developed states registered a faster increase in their gross state domestic product (GSDP) than the less developed ones. Since the growth in gross domestic product (GDP) in the post-reform period has been driven largely by the growth in the services sector, certain states well-endowed in respect of industrial infrastructure and financial services could achieve higher growth rates in GSDP. The decline in the rate of public investment in infrastructure in the post-reform period is basically responsible for this divergence in growth rates as, a rise in such public investment would have favoured the less developed states. The same divergence in the pattern of investment and growth may hold true as between different regions within certain larger states. The continuing, and even accentuating, regional tensions within some of these states bear testimony to such developments.

The Eleventh Plan claims to outline "a comprehensive programme for development of infrastructure, especially in rural areas, and in the remote and backward parts of the country consistent with the requirements of inclusive growth at 9 per cent per year" (Planning Commission, 2008). But from the information given in the Plan document, it is not possible to find out how the infrastructure planned is going to be spread over different states, on the one hand and between agriculture and the non-farm sector including small towns, on the other.

The growth rates actually achieved during the Tenth Plan in the less developed states like Bihar, Madhya Pradesh, Rajasthan and Uttar Pradesh fell considerably short of the targets. The targeted growth rates of GSDP for the Eleventh Plan do show smaller divergence between the richer and poorer states than those achieved in the Tenth Plan. But the absence of targets in respect of investment rates casts doubt on the credibility of these growth targets.

There is no basis to believe that the divergence in the investment rates between the poor and better-off states would come down in the Eleventh Plan period. For one thing, as discussed in Chapter 4, the per capita plan outlays of the poorer states have been declining relative to those of the richer states in the post-reform period and private investment has been flowing basically to the high income states where infrastructure is well developed owing to higher per capita plan outlays. There is no increase in central assistance in the Eleventh Plan for infrastructure development of the backward regions through Backward Regions Grant Fund, Special Plan for Bihar and Action Plan for the undivided KBK (Kalahandi-Bolangir-Koraput districts of Orissa), which have only been protected at the Tenth Plan level. Such assistance constitutes less than 1 per cent of total Eleventh Plan outlay for all states.

In view of the steep decline in public investment, the Planning Commission suggests that states should focus on providing the necessary policy framework and supporting environment to attract private sector investments (Planning Commission, 2008). But, can such a 'supporting environment' make good the gaps in public investment in infrastructure? As noted in Chapter 1, historically, due to the differences in land tenure systems and other factors, the developed states have had relatively more efficient systems of governance in terms of skills, responsiveness and the quality of delivery systems (See also World Bank, 2006). Therefore, while many of the suggested measures for 'good governance' are desirable, they cannot be a substitute for the provision of adequate infrastructure through public investment. There is a case for revisiting the whole area of infrastructure development in the less developed regions and the rural areas in general.

There is, however, a silver lining in the more recent experience. As shown in the last chapter, the newly created smaller states, *viz.*, Uttarakhand, Jharkhand and Chhattisgarh have achieved much higher growth rates in their GSDP than the targets set for the Tenth Five Year Plan, whereas the growth rates achieved by their parent states, *viz.*, Uttar Pradesh, Bihar and Madhya Pradesh fell significantly short of the targets. Further, the growth rates achieved in the first two years of the Eleventh Plan, i.e., 2007-08 and 2008-09, by Chhattisgarh and Uttarakhand were significantly higher than those achieved by their parent states. Apart from releasing the creative energies of the people, viability of smaller states may have contributed to better governance, attracting greater private investment from outside as well as planning and utilising resources more efficiently (World Bank, 2007).

An extremely encouraging development is in respect of Bihar, where the average growth rate achieved at 9.7 per cent per annum during these two years was significantly higher than for Jharkhand at 5.8 per cent per annum (Aiyar, 2010; Rao, 2010). This may be explained by improved governance, of late, in this state, facilitated not the least by the fact that with the creation of Jharkhand, Bihar has become less heterogeneous and much smaller in area, with the size of its population getting reduced by about 25 per cent.

The need to reduce inter-state and intra-state disparities in development has emerged as one of the biggest challenges in the post-reform period. Major initiatives from the Planning Commission are called for to bridge the infrastructural gaps by mobilising massive public and private investments for the less developed areas; to restructure the institutions for the management of infrastructure and to initiate reforms in governance. To ensure greater accountability for the development of backward regions in bigger states, it may be desirable to constitute Regional Development Boards and, where necessary, to carve out separate states comprising some of the backward regions.

Experience has, however, demonstrated the failure of regional planning to ensure adequate development of backward regions within the larger states. This is explained by the politics of planning in democracy inherent in such states characterised by regional unevenness in development. The experience of Maharashtra and Gujarat amply illustrates the failure to develop backward regions, despite the existence of constitutional provisions for setting up Regional Planning Boards and the powers entrusted to the Governor to review the progress of development under such regional plans. This experience underlines the need for conceding separate statehood for certain backward regions like Telangana and Vidarbha.

The observations of B.R. Ambedkar, the principal architect of our Constitution, on the desirability of smaller states are prophetic (Ambedkar, 1979). He welcomed the recommendation of the States Reorganisation Commission in 1955 for the creation of Hyderabad state consisting of Telangana region and creation of Vidarbha as a separate state. Further, he envisaged the division of Uttar Pradesh into three states (Western, Central and Eastern); Bihar into two (North and South or present Jharkhand); Madhya Pradesh into two (Northern and Southern) and Maharashtra into three (Western, Central and Eastern). He was for linguistic homogeneity of a state in the sense of 'one state-one language' and not 'one language-one state'. He thus envisaged two Telugu speaking states, three Marathi speaking states and a large number of Hindi speaking states.

While arguing for smaller states, Ambedkar was guided basically by two considerations. One, no single state should be large enough to exercise undue influence in the federation. Drawing from the American experience, he thought that smaller states were in the best interests of healthy federalism. On this issue, his views were similar to those of K.M. Panikkar, set out in his note of dissent to the Report of the States Reorganisation Commission. Second, he thought that socially disadvantaged sections are likely to be subjected to greater discrimination in bigger states because of the consolidation of socially privileged or dominant groups.

Over the last half a century, two new dimensions have been added. Population growth and the multiplicity of developmental functions have rendered governance in large size states inefficient. Secondly, as argued in Chapter 5, in the context of development planning under democracy, significant regional diversities with respect to the historically inherited levels of infrastructure and institutions within certain large states have given rise to severe tensions concerning the distribution of benefits from development. These tensions have reached a point where harmonious development seems no longer possible without their break-up into smaller stares which are relatively homogeneous.

The essays in this book on "Regional Disparities, Smaller States and Statehood for Telangana" were written on different occasions over the last four decades since 1969. These are being reproduced in view of renewed interest in the subject in the context of emerging regional tensions and the revival of the demands for the creation of smaller states.

References

Ambedkar, Babasaheb (1979). *Writings and Speeches,* Vol.I (Part II-On Linguistic States). Education Department, Government of Maharashtra.

Aiyar, Swaminathan S. Anklesaria (2010). "Fast Growth Trickles Up from the States". *Economic Times,* January 6.

Planning Commission (2008). *Eleventh Five Year Plan (2007-2012),* Vol.I. Government of India, New Delhi.

Rao, C.H.H. (2010). "Statehood for Telangana", *Economic Times,* January 9.

World Bank (2006). *Inclusive Growth and Service Delivery: Building on India's Success.* World Bank Development Policy Review. Macmillan India Ltd.

———. (2007). *Jharkhand: Addressing the Challenges of Inclusive Development, Rural Poverty and Economic Management.* India Country Management Unit, South Asia.

Section I

Regional Disparities

1 Poverty and Development
Characteristics of Less-Developed Regions in India

Ever since the advent of economic planning in India, three distinct strategies for economic development and alleviation of poverty have been advocated. During the first two decades of planning, the planners and policymakers emphasised the need to maximise the rate of growth of GNP by stepping up the rate of investment in the economy. Public investment in physical infrastructure was considered a prerequisite for stimulating private investment. It was felt that the growth of GNP, by itself, would take care of poverty to a considerable extent. There was the structural school which advocated radical redistribution of assets through land reforms and nationalisation of big industries, etc. According to this school, neither growth nor improved distribution could be possible without such a redistribution. During the 1970s, the disillusionment with the strategy of maximising growth in GNP gave rise to the idea of a direct attack on poverty through rural development, small industries and labour-intensive techniques, minimum needs programme, group-oriented and employment-oriented programme such as SFDA, MFAL, etc. The Antyodaya scheme, according to which a few poorest families within each village are chosen for programmes to uplift them, is an extreme case of this strategy of direct attack on poverty.

For a large country like India with enormous regional disparities in development and differences in the institutional framework deriving, in quite a few cases, from cultural diversities, any single strategy for the whole country may not prove to be appropriate. For the less-developed regions in the country, the strategy to maximise growth through regional development may need to dominate while a direct attack on poverty may have to be given priority in some of the developed regions. Structural changes may become a necessary prerequisite in certain other regions for stimulating growth as well as for ensuring better distribution. Moreover, all the three strategies seem to underplay the vital role of factors such as entrepreneurship, administration, constraints and possibilities arising from the particular cultural framework, the bargaining power of the less-developed regions and of the less-privileged groups, etc. Therefore, an understanding of the characteristic feature of different regions of the country may be necessary for identifying strategies and policies suitable for different regions and for incorporating further useful elements into the known strategies.

We propose to make an attempt in this direction in this paper. Our observations are in the nature of reflections or loud thinking and are based upon impressions during visits to these areas and on discussions with different sections of people.

Vertical disparities (i.e., between different income groups) perceived at the national or macro level derive, to a significant extent, from the horizontal (or regional) disparities because the less-developed regions, where the poor predominate, account for a large part of the population below the poverty line in the country. When confronted with such less-developed regions, one is struck by these horizontal disparities which appear sharper than the vertical disparities within such regions. Therefore, in such cases, the development of the region as a whole through the first type of strategy is likely to contribute significantly to the reduction of poverty. That is to say, the reduction of horizontal disparities in itself would contribute significantly to the reduction of vertical disparities at the national level. In fact, so far as these less-developed regions are concerned, a direct attack on poverty would mean the development of the regions as a whole. Schemes like Antyodaya may not be effective, for example, in regions where the whole area is affected by salinity, or where there is little or no water for irrigation.

The regions discussed in this note are: (i) Azamgarh district in East UP which is typical of the poorer regions in the Gangetic plains; (ii) Tripura representing special problems of the border area with low resource base and mass in-migration; (iii) Chotanagpur-Santhal Parganas and tribal Orissa which represent the southern belt of eastern zone with special characteristics of their own; (iv) Jhabua, the tribal district of Madhya

Pradesh, which represents the backward but fast moving or dynamic parts of Central India; (v) Jodhpur-Jaisalmer area which is among the most dry and arid tracts of the country; and (vi) Kalpa (Himachal Pradesh) and Ladakh (Jammu and Kashmir), the snowy Himalayan regions on the northern border. These six regions can be broadly grouped into three based upon some common characteristics. East UP and Tripura are characterised by heavy demographic pressure and many of their problems of poverty and destitution arise from this feature. The areas predominated by tribal population, e.g., Chotanagpur-Santhal Parganas, tribal Orissa and Jhabua share common problems arising from the distinctiveness of their culture; and both the desert regions of Rajasthan and snowy Himalayan tracts are characterised by the sparsity of population, long distances, difficult terrain and consequently very high cost for the provision of infrastructure when compared to other regions.

On the basis of our explorations, we identify five major characteristics of these regions as most relevant for our discussion. These are: (1) poor resource base and poor infrastructure; (2) low levels of living and lack of enterprise; (3) misallocation of public resources; (4) deficiencies in administration; and (5) weaker bargaining power.

Poor Resource Base and Poor Infrastructure

East UP and Tripura present the case of extreme pressure of population on the scarce resources available. Whereas this has resulted in the out-migration of labour on a significant scale from East UP, the pressure in Tripura is the result of large-scale in-migration of population from Bangladesh. The poor resource base in these regions, despite the existence of considerable exploitable potential, is essentially attributable to deficiency of public investment in the infrastructure, because the exploitation of the potentially available resources as well as returns from private effort depend crucially on the availability of infrastructure.

In the areas of East UP visited, salinity or *usar* and floods are the main problems because of which the enormous groundwater potential remains unexploited and investment in agriculture seems to be inhibited owing to low return, as well as uncertainty of returns. From Azamgarh to Varanasi, for example, one finds that at least 75 per cent of the area has become unfit for cultivation owing to salinity. Its reclamation requires community effort and substantial investment in gypsum and water. Both of them are beyond the means of individual cultivators. Without public subsidy for the provisions of gypsum as well as exploitation of groundwater through large-scale investment in public tube wells and big administrative effort to reclaim land and arrest floods through community effort, it would not be possible to make agriculture remunerative. Rural electrification has to accompany such efforts to stimulate enterprise in agriculture.

In Tripura, owing to large-scale in-migration of population from Bangladesh with which it has a long border, the proportions of tribal and non-tribal population have been reversed within a short period. The proportion of tribal population has been reduced from 70 per cent to 30 per cent while that of non-tribals, consisting mainly of refugees, has become 70 per cent. This is the position according to 1971 Census and the proportion of non-tribals has undoubtedly increased further in the subsequent period. Tripura has thus become almost a mirror of Bangladesh.

The majority of migrants are destitutes, so that Tripura today is probably the poorest state in India. The pressure of population is so great that even tribals are becoming increasingly responsive to family planning practices. The pressure on resources has led to felling of trees and deforestation on a significant scale. The bamboo material is important next only to land and is used to the maximum for buildings, equipment and impressive handicrafts. The cycle for *jhum* or shifting cultivation is coming down rapidly, because of population pressure, resulting in lower productivity per unit of land. Jackfruit seems to be the only plentiful resource but its price is very much lower than in Bangladesh because of a ban on its export. However, despite the talk of prohibition, research is being conducted with public support on how to brew liquor from this plentiful jackfruit.

The paucity of resources is dramatised by the fact that there is hardly any building worth the name for the judiciary to sit. Tripura has very often been called a police state but there are hardly any buildings for housing the police! Moreover, because of the extensive use of bamboo material, the annual cost of repairs is very high for the existing public dwellings.

There are no large farmers in Tripura owning more than 10 acres. Partition proved to be an important contributing factor for the success of land reforms in this part of the country. The per capita land is hardly 15 cents and as many as 80 per cent of farmers own less than 2 acres. Land alienation has been declared illegal since 1960. Despite this, the alienation of land from tribals to non-tribal refugees continues. However, these refugees themselves being destitutes, the alienation could be more a result of cultural factors than of economic exploitation. On the whole, therefore, one gets a picture of overall regional backwardness rather than of any significant inequalities within the region.

In the tribal belts of Chotanagpur-Santhal Parganas and Orissa, the poor resource base is attributable not merely to paucity of investible resources for exploiting the potential but also importantly to the motivation and the institutional framework of tribal population. These areas are fertile, rich in natural resources, and people are hardworking and yet the transition from the modes of work and living of tribal societies to those of the rest seems to be slow. Therefore, adaptation to new techniques of production and modes of living seems to be as important as financial resources.

For instance, in much of the Chotanagpur-Santhal Parganas, where tank irrigation is not possible due to high evaporation, there is considerable scope for lift irrigation from river beds. Consequently, dug-wells have become popular but with as high a public subsidy as 75 per cent. Manual labour is quite common for lift irrigation. People are found to carry very heavy articles on their heads and shoulders for which bullock carts are normally used elsewhere. Soils are rich and nature is kind but the people, despite their hard work, are poor because of low level of technological development, which itself may be attributed to inadequate extension effort as well as to the slow response of tribal population to innovations.

The position is somewhat different in the tribal district of Jhabua in Madhya Pradesh where there is a great demand for public investment in irrigation. This is understandable in view of the frequent occurrence of droughts, low soil cover and consequently low moisture content of soil. Tribals (Bhils) constitute 85 per cent of the population in this district. Due to population pressure and lack of irrigation, the encroachment on forests has been so severe that most forest land was cut up 10 years ago. The undulating terrain of this district makes tank irrigation possible in a large number of places. Yet, scarcity of water for irrigation and drinking is the most important problem in the area. Tribals themselves come forward to tell spontaneously how more irrigation is possible through the construction of tanks in places cited by them.

In all these areas, especially in Santhal Parganas, there is little landlessness despite the alienation of land from tribals to non-tribals, so that not much inequality is visible among these communities. Poverty is, of course, widespread and is more acute than in East UP where remittances from migrants constitute an important source of income.

In the regions characterised by sparsity of population and long distances, difficult terrain and adverse climatic conditions, e.g., Jodhpur-Jaisalmer area in Rajasthan, Kalpa in Himachal Pradesh and Ladakh in Jammu and Kashmir, the poor resource base is attributable in a large measure to the very high cost of the provision of infrastructure. Beyond a point, without the availability of cheap and abundant sources of energy, the provision of infrastructure in these areas would prove to be very costly. One would thus look for the most sophisticated technology to lift up the areas characterised by the most primitive conditions.

Water is the scarcest resource in Jodhpur-Jaisalmer area—the driest tract of Rajasthan. The impurities in the available drinking water result in the widespread incidence of water-borne diseases, e.g., paralysis of limbs and legs, etc. The scarcity of water is dramatised in stories of how mothers-in-law tease their daughters-in-law for attempting to take a bath on every festival or how mothers of even 10-12 children have never seen their hair wet in their lifetime. Traditional methods of water-harvesting and water-storage are exploited fully. Due to the scarcity of water and fodder and to population pressure, significant changes are taking place in the structure of livestock; cattle are fast giving place to sheep and goats. There are fodder banks storing fodder for 5-6 years. With a little more of drinking water, more animals can be reared because of the abundance of dry grass.

There is a great demand for more buildings for officers in the interior areas, for more roads, electricity, schools, hospitals, police stations, etc. This is because, economies of scale are absent in the provision of infrastructure in this area as the villages are of small size and are separated by long distances.

The problems are essentially the same in the snowy Himalayan regions. The areas in the interior like Lahaul and Spiti are not accessible for 8-9 months in a year and are, therefore, even more backward than Kinnaur in Kalpa district. Landslides and avalanches are frequent which breach roads and the irrigation channels and cause floods. The cost of construction and maintenance of roads and irrigation channels is, therefore, very high. Transportation of apples on headloads is a common phenomenon because of bad roads and non-availability of commercial transport. Though snowy, these tracts are dry for all practical purposes because of very scanty rainfall. There are a number of *kuhls* (irrigation channels whose source is melting snow or glaciers) but they are damaged because of avalanches. Repairs of existing *kuhls* would appear to cost approximately Rs. 500 per irrigated hectare as against Rs. 7,000 per irrigated hectare for the construction of new *kuhls*, for which there is a significant potential. Beyond Kalpa at Pooh at the height of 9,000 to 12,000 ft, where there is hardly any vegetation, there is considerable demand as well as potential for irrigation from *kuhls*. It is amazing that in the lap of Himalayas amidst snow rocks, irrigation is rated as the most important problem by village *pradhans*, officials and non-officials alike. Their order of priority is: irrigation, roads, hospitals, schools and drinking water.

Ladakh with about 1 lakh population but accounting for half the area of Jammu and Kashmir presents the same picture of dry weather with scanty rainfall and vegetation and deficiency of oxygen. The lush green patches found here and there indicate the very high productivity of water. One is struck by the sight of tomatos weighing 10-15 kilos each and radishes of the human size. Ladakh which is one of the coldest spots on the earth suffers from severe droughts as well as floods. Lack of communications is the most important problem but the cost of their provision is prohibitive because of long distances as well as high cost of material. For example, price of cement rises as one goes up because of transportation costs. Its cost in Ladakh is 50 per cent higher than in Jammu and Kashmir and about 100 per cent higher than in the rest of the country.

Low Levels of Living and Lack of Enterprise

Any comparison of 'levels of living' across regions with populations of diverse cultures suffers from the limitation that it is difficult to take account of the subjective valuations of people concerned regarding what constitutes a 'reasonable' level of living. However, in the less-developed regions, the basic necessities of life are far from satisfactory and the desire for improvement is universal, so that such a comparison would still be useful. In these comparisons, level of living is judged by the availability of basic goods and services such as food, clothing, housing, medical and schooling facilities, etc. Some of the 'poorer' communities may nevertheless be 'rich' in their cultures. In fact, beauty and poverty are very often found to co-exist. Also, if one comes across people who are very courteous, warm-hearted and hospitable, one can rest assured that their per capita income must be much below the national average!

The poor resource base arising from insufficient exploitation of the available potential in the less-developed regions is responsible for the low level of per capita income, lower wages, malnutrition, diseases from malnutrition as well as from non-availability of proper drinking water. These regions are also characterised by poor schooling and health facilities, insufficient and badly maintained roads because of paucity of public resources. Except in Tripura where poverty is largely the consequence of in-migration, and in Chotanagpur-Santhal Parganas and tribal Orissa where tribal values and institutions are important in explaining the insufficient exploitation of the potential, the rest of the less-developed regions visited, *viz.*, Azamgarh, Jhabua, Jodhpur-Jaisalmer, Kalpa and Ladakh are characterised by out-migration of population in varying degrees for varying periods. This underscores the importance of labour-intensive techniques in the 'labour-scarce' developed regions and horizontal flow of incomes from the developed to the less developed regions, for reducing poverty. This also emphasises the importance of raising output, particularly the food grains output, in the less developed regions for raising the nutritional levels and for combating diseases arising from the shortage of food.

Apart from malnutrition, quite a few people in these regions seem to be suffering from water-borne diseases, rendering them weak and lethargic. The lack of enterprise on their part as labourers or family farm workers could well be mistaken by the observers for their lack of economic motivation or 'other worldliness', because they are not found to be putting in as much hard labour as their counterparts in the better-off regions.

Interviews with a large cross-section of people in Azamgarh suggests that between 20 and 25 per cent of population must have migrated outside. Muslims migrate as bakers to Malaysia and Hindus generally as farm labourers to Punjab. It appears that as much as 40 per cent of disposable income in this area could be attributed to remittances, mostly from Punjab. Despite such large remittances spent on consumption, the area is distinctly poor. Actual wage rate in rural areas is as low as Rs. 2.50 per day as against the statutory minimum wage of Rs. 5 per day. Even harvest wages do not seem to exceed Rs. 3.00. This provides an opportunity for contractors to make extra profits from public works, to the extent of the difference between the statutory minimum and the actual wage.

In the tribal belts of Chotanagpur-Santhal Parganas, Orissa and Jhabua, one does not get the same picture of destitution as in Tripura, partly because the demographic pressure is not so intense and also because the food habits of the tribal populations allow for better nourishment. However, they appear underclothed which may be attributable, in part, to their habits. The wages are slightly higher than in East UP or Tripura. In Santhal Parganas, cash wages range between Rs. 2.50 and 3.00 per day in addition to the breakfast provided by the employer, while the price of rice ranges between Rs. 1.10 and Rs. 1.75 per kilo. In tribal Orissa, the wages range between Rs. 3 and Rs. 4 per day.

Thus, as one moves from the eastern plains characterised by high demographic pressure to the tribal belts, one finds people slightly better fed but underclothed, participating in harder physical labour with little use of bullocks. Also, the inequality in the levels of living among these people appears less than in the eastern plains which, again, may be attributed to the egalitarian character of tribal institutions.

People in Kalpa (HP) look poor, undernourished and, considering the harder climate, very much ill-clothed. They, however, possess beauty in ample measure and are humble, innocent and warm-hearted. The per capita production of food grains in this region is about half the average per capita level in the state. For about nine months in a year, the people are cut off even from their *tehsil* headquarters. Transportation of food grains in this period is done by using goats because mule tracks are closed. Thus, the number of goats available limits the quantity of food grains available. The supply of goats is itself dependent on the availability of pastures and grass. Milk powder is used by the very few who can afford it. Due to severe malnutrition, the incidence of tuberculosis is very high, about 60 per cent of population being affected by this disease. The institution of polyandry among Kinnauris as well as among the Ladakhis, which is now breaking down under the impact of modernisation, appears to have been a method of adjustment of population to the low means of subsistence. With the breakdown of this institution and the emergence of monogamy, however, the dependency ratio has increased steeply accentuating the problem of malnutrition and disease.

Wage rates in these far-flung Himalayan regions are high because of higher cost of living. In Ladakh actual or market wages range between Rs. 10 and 15 per day as against the statutorily fixed minimum wage of Rs. 6 per day. Because of this, there is no incentive for local labour to work in construction and other public works. Contractors bring labour from Bihar and Nepal and other places where the wage rates are low.

Minimum statutory wages need to be raised at least to the level of actual market wages obtaining in these areas for generating more employment and income among the local people. Public distribution of subsidised food grains is essential in these areas to improve nutrition. However, the development of irrigation through the repairs of existing *kuhls* and the construction of new ones, for which there is considerable scope, needs to be given the highest priority because it is difficult for the supplies of food grains from outside to reach the areas in the interior during the greater part of the year. The development of irrigation would thus have the greatest impact in the fight against malnutrition and disease in these areas.

All the regions visited are characterised by the lack of entrepreneurship. Also, the labour force appears to lack vitality and enterprise. The absence of entrepreneurship in certain regions, particularly in the tribal belt, is explained by the institutional factors. The low investible surplus and the non-availability of infrastructure resulting in low as well as high uncertainty of returns are the major factors in certain other regions. For instance, the Jodhpur-Jaisalmer area of Rajasthan is the home of some of the leading entrepreneurs in the country who have accomplished a great deal outside the region but find themselves helpless in their home region. Malnutrition and disease could be responsible for the lack of vitality and dexterity and consequently low productivity of labour in these regions. The migrant workers from East UP are, however, known to be quite enterprising in their places of work partly because generally, the more enterprising ones migrate outside and also because their earnings are attractive and they can meet their minimum consumption requirements. The lack of enterprise in the less-developed regions is responsible for the low credit-deposit ratios reported by the banking institutions in many of these regions implying an outflow of investible resources.

The development of infrastructure through public investment is a necessary condition for stimulating entrepreneurship in some of these regions. This would need to be supplemented by the provision of institutional finance on liberal terms. However, for quite some time, the gap will have to be filled by the public sector enterprises. This raises the problems of allocational and administrative efficiency and of organisation.

Misallocation of Public Resources

Before we discuss the allocation of public resources in the less-developed regions, it is necessary to note a very favourable factor contributing to efficiency in the use of scarce capital resources in the eastern Gangetic plains which are characterised by the abundance of labour and low wages. The capital-labour ratio appears to be low in these areas which, by itself, could give a lower capital-output ratio. However, it is important to ensure that the effect of this favourable factor is not neutralised, or counter-balanced by the other unfavourable factors causing misallocation of resources.

The allocational problems in the less-developed regions range from outright leakages of funds due to corruption which reduce the investible resources, to the very high capital-output ratios. These problems may be listed as follows: (i) leakages of resources; (ii) ostentation in public services; (iii) neglect of existing assets; (iv) investments in projects which have little or no linkages with the economy of the region; and (v) tendency to spend on salaries rather than on the creation of capital assets, particularly in areas where capital-output ratios are very high.

One hears more about corruption and leakages of public funds in the less-developed regions where resources for investment are needed most. This is no doubt an outcome of a general desire for quick gains. The absence of entrepreneurship and a strong middle class and excessive dependence on bureaucracy are also responsible for this malady. Therefore, there are no easy or quick solutions for getting out of this vicious circle of under-development. However, greater decentralisation of authority with greater devolution of functions to village *panchayats* can serve as a check on the leakages of funds by providing mass vigilance.

Ostentation in public services is particularly visible in areas characterised historically by *zamindari* tenure or in tribal belts where there is practically no middle class. The district officers have to receive a number of dignitories frequently which not only dislocates the normal administrative work but also involves lavish expenditure on the hospitality provided to them.

There is widespread demand throughout the country for investments in irrigation, roads, schools, hospitals, etc. This is understandable in a developing economy with democratic framework. However, this has also led to the diversion of resources from the maintenance of existing assets (e.g., buildings, roads, etc.), which is a non-Plan item, to fresh investments under the Plans. It is true that this implies, in general, a redistribution of resources to the new areas, particularly the rural sector, and to the relatively poorer sections. But beyond a point, this practice results in huge losses on account of the deterioration of existing assets. It appears that in large parts of the country the benefits to the society from the given extra expenditure on the maintenance of existing assets could be greater than from the same amount spent on the creation of new assets.

The tendency to neglect the maintenance of existing assets is even more glaring in the less-developed regions, because of paucity of resources and greater demands for new works under the plan as well as for increased salaries for the establishment. The position becomes worse when the cost of maintenance is higher. For instance, in the Chotanagpur-Santhal

Parganas because of high rainfall and slopy land, water does not hold and the roads are easily damaged. In this area, the roofs of several school buildings are found to be leaking so profusely that umbrellas have to be used inside the buildings. Same is the case with quite a few hospital buildings. It is estimated that about 40 per cent of school buildings in this area are without roof. This must be having an unhealthy impact on the psychology of school-going children at their impressionable age. Office buildings constructed only a decade ago look 50 years old because there is virtually no maintenance or repairs of these buildings. Visible poverty can attract sympathy and consideration, but if this leads to a vested interest in poverty, the barriers to its removal would indeed become strong.

The position is somewhat different in areas visited in Madhya Pradesh where social services are not well developed and the financial constraint is not severe. There is a genuine desire to curtail expenditure on salaries and to embark upon new constructions. Because of the low-wage economy and fewer existing assets, there is a significant saving on non-Plan account. These areas have a considerable capacity to absorb investment in irrigation, roads, schools, hospitals, etc., under the Plan.

Many of the projects located in South Bihar and Orissa have little or no linkages with the economy of the regions concerned. This is attributable, in part, to the particular institutional framework characterised by feudal tendencies and customs and the absence of entrepreneurship and the middle class. There is abundance of mineral wealth in South Bihar and yet mining is done predominantly by non-tribal labour drawn from Bihar as well as from other parts of the country. According to some officers familiar with tribal institutions, the location of giant industrial enterprises and the modernisation of agriculture at a rapid pace would bypass a large majority of local population with little impact on their levels of living. Development of small enterprises based upon local material wherever possible and with adequate training in skills for local population would have a better impact in transforming their lives.

In the Himalayan regions, there is a great demand for jobs with the government because the alternative sources of earnings are very meagre, highly seasonal and uncertain. Because of higher cost of living, the salary levels have to be higher than in the plains. The cost of construction is very high in these areas. Also, traditionally and culturally, these communities are not saving- and investment-oriented. Consequently, there is a clear tendency for public expenditure to flow into salaries and current income rather than into investment. It is felt by many that unless the transfer of resources is earmarked for specific projects, it would be difficult to break the vicious circle of under-development and ever expanding bureaucracy in these regions.

Deficiencies in Administration

Across states, one finds a clear correlation between the level of economic development and the status enjoyed by the bureaucracy *vis-a-vis* the politician. In the less-developed states and regions, especially in the eastern zone, bureaucracy seems to have been reduced to a passive intermediary between the politicians and the people. There is little display of initiative either in giving advice to the politicians or in implementing the programmes. Unlike in the developed states, the attitude of servility towards the politician seems obvious in these areas. Similarly, politicians do not seem to show bureaucracy the respect and consideration it deserves. Apart from the general lack of social motivation and initiative, particularly in ex-*zamindari* areas, there is alienation from or lack of identification with the backward regions, especially within larger states marked by regional disparities. Superimposed on these limitations is the lack of infrastructure, e.g., roads, buildings, etc., in the sparsely populated states which discourages the flow of administrative talent into the interior areas.

The supply lines are particularly inelastic in larger states. In Azamgarh area, for instance, people were told that hundreds of bags of gypsum had been released from Lucknow. The people concerned shuttled between major towns for several months to receive the material but without success. The consequences of administrative deficiencies become serious and glaring in the sensitive sectors like the long border between Tripura and Bangladesh where there is frequent lifting of cattle, felling of trees and smuggling. In the absence of adequate personnel to man the long border, scare is created occasionally by shooting down the criminals.

In South Bihar where density is relatively less, *tolas* or hamlets with 10-15 families each are separated by a radius of about 10 miles. This renders the provision of social services costly. Moreover, there is no incentive for the officers to stay in these areas because of lack of amenities. In Santhal Parganas, about 30 per cent of vacancies in medical posts were reported to be unfilled because of the reluctance of the doctors to go to the interiors. Paradoxically, administration is found satisfactory where officers from outside the region dominate. Those belonging to the region and hence with a better knowledge and sense of identification with the region are, however, debilitated by caste and factional antagonisms and are usually more effective outside their own region.

Himalayan regions suffer from all the disadvantages mentioned: sparsity of population, long distances, difficult terrain and lack of amenities. Kalpa region, for example, has produced several civil servants who have held high positions in HP but hardly any one would be willing to serve in the area because of inaccessibility, little amenities and high cost of living. The officers in the area are cut off from their families for several months in winter. Even the incentive allowance of 125 per cent now given has not been able to attract them because they have to maintain two establishments, one at the headquarters, usually in Simla, and another at the place of assignment. The more influential ones among officers manage to get out of the area. The less-influential and the incompetent alone remain and being frustrated all the time, prove to be more a liability than an instrument of service. Because of this alienation on the part of outside officers, often the relatively less qualified but experienced local officers are able to suggest useful innovations for the solution of problems.

It is significant that most of the states with less-developed regions, e.g., UP, Bihar, MP, Rajasthan, HP and J&K are either large in terms of area or very sparsely populated. Constitution of smaller states wherever viable could improve administration enormously. Greater representation to the tribals and others from the backward regions in services could make administration more alive to the local conditions and responsive to their needs. Greater devolution of functions to the local institutions such as *panchayats* would also be helpful, particularly in situations of inaccessibility to public services. Also, there needs to be greater dependence on intermediate skills for medical and engineering services, etc., through appropriate training of local talent.

Weaker Bargaining Power

Since the less-developed regions are characterised by poor resource base, the issue of transfer of investible resources to these regions from the Centre or from the developed regions seems to evoke greater concern than the redistribution of the existing resources between different classes. Consequently, the unrest takes the form of Centre-state conflict when the state as a whole is poor or regional conflict in cases where the less-developed and the developed regions co-exist within the same state. Such states usually plead for more resources from the Centre in the name of the less-developed regions. If the conflicts are not sharp at present in certain cases, it is because of insufficient awareness and lack of bargaining power.

The densely populated eastern plains have contributed eminent leaders both at the state and Central level ever since Independence but the per capita transfer of resources to these areas has been lower than the national average. The most charitable but somewhat vain explanation for this phenomenon is that these leaders being too big, placed the national interests above those of their regions. But a more persuasive explanation given by some very perceptive scholars is that because of the feudal and aristocratic background, the leaders of these regions were not interested in development. This view is also held by no less a leader than Jayaprakash Narayan. It is also probable that in view of the constraints imposed by the social structure in this area, some of these leaders could accomplish much more outside their own home states.

However, people in general in the eastern plains appear militant, though poor. They are politically conscious and are bold enough to voice their demands and challenge the false statistics of achievement paraded by the officials in their presence. From this, one finds a confirmation of the hypothesis that this area was probably neglected by the British because of its militant role in the freedom struggle.

In the tribal belts of Chotanagpur-Santhal Parganas and Orissa, the people are hardworking but are passive and even docile. About one-third of MLAs in Bihar belong to South Bihar. The representation to Adivasis in higher services is 10 per cent and there are now a couple of Adivasi IAS officers. Yet, their impact on regional development is not significant. Alienation of land from the tribals to the non-tribal inmigrants continues to be the most important problem. Despite legislation banning such alienation, about 30 per cent of land stands alienated to those from North Bihar. Two or three non-tribal families can dominate the entire tribal village. Some tribals even refuse to take back land because of the commitments made to the moneylenders by their forefathers.

The same is the case in large parts of Orissa where economic motivation as well as resistance to injustices is weak. The more enterprising farmers from Andhra are able to occupy their lands after working as tenants for some time. Because of these motivational and institutional reasons, there is no assurance that tribal areas will get their due share out of resources transferred to the states from the Centre on account of tribal development.

In the Himalayan regions there has been some growth of middle class but it is essentially pampered from above. They are, therefore, parasitic and corrupt. They evince little interest in local problems. The demand for carving out a separate district of Kargil instead of remaining a part of Ladakh has been prompted essentially because of the neglect of the region by this parasitic leadership.

Spread of education and reservation in services, particularly for the tribals, is necessary for raising the overall bargaining power of the less-developed regions. Separate statehood for the less-developed regions located in larger states could turn out to be a decisive factor in their development. In cases where such regions are non-viable as states, separate Regional Development Councils with greater autonomy can serve the same purpose. It is necessary to devolve functions, as far as possible, to the village *panchayats* and thus raise the initiative of the people for preventing the growth of parasitic middle class and for curbing its power.

Development can be rapid in the eastern region if adequate transfer of resources is accompanied by reorganisation. In view of the demographic pressure as well as the existence of significant exploitable potential, resource transfer needs to be substantial for these regions. The discontent because of slow growth is also likely to be greatest in these areas. Hilly and desert regions are also dynamic but the transfer of resources needs to be commensurate with high cost of construction and of provision of services. Local initiative needs to be raised in the remote regions together with stationing of competent officers. In the tribal belt the process of change is bound to be slower. In any case, it is necessary to arrest the growth of parasitic middle class and evolve mechanisms for the adaptation of development pattern to tribal institutions and vice-versa.

In view of the diversity and complexity of the problems of regional development, it is necessary to have a standing National Commission on Regional Development for constantly reviewing the pattern of resource transfer to these areas in the light of the recommendations of the Finance Commission and Planning Commission; to assemble the necessary data on regional levels of development; to review the progress of development; and to explore innovations, organisational and otherwise, for greater transfer of resources as well as for their better absorption. The work done by such a National Commission on a continuing basis could considerably strengthen the bargaining power of the less-developed regions where a significant part of the country's poor live.

Economic and Political Weekly XIV(30, 31 & 32), Special Number, August 1979.

2 Planning for Development and Removal of Regional Imbalances with Special Reference to Bihar

There are disparities within the country as between different states and also between various regions within states. There are a number of developed states where there are pockets of backwardness or low level of regional development. There are states like Bihar where almost the whole state is less developed or backward economically by any standard.

Today, if a developed state which ranks number 1, number 2 or number 3 in the country, also has some less developed pockets, then it is not so much due to lack of resources, it is essentially due to inefficient allocation of resources. A richer state which has sufficient surpluses after meeting its revenue expenditure or non-plan expenditure, is potentially in a position to remove backwardness of some of its areas. But, if after decades of economic development, these areas continued to be very backward, it only suggests that the resources have not been properly allocated. The position really becomes serious in the case of states like Bihar where almost the entire state is economically backward or UP where except certain parts, like western part, a large area continued to remain backward whether it is hill areas or eastern UP or Bundelkhand. These states are short of resources. Let me say at the very outset that the resources are only one of the factors accounting for backwardness and development. There are many other factors apart from resources such as technology, organisation and institutions which are important in trying to understand backwardness and factors which promote development. But there is no doubt about the fact that in many of the less developed states where less developed regions predominate, there is resource constraint.

If we look at the country as a whole and survey the growth in the last 30 years of planning, there is no doubt that we are confronted with sharp regional disparities. One region which stands out prominently consists of almost the whole of eastern Gangetic plains extending from UP and Bihar, West Bengal and parts of Tripura and several other northeastern states. This region has lagged behind very much in the growth rate when compared to the country as a whole. This does not mean that these regions have not benefitted at all or have not grown at all in the last 30 years. There has been significant improvement in irrigation, power and social development. And, income has grown faster than the population, which was not so in the pre-Independence period. These regions have grown but certainly the rate of growth of these regions has very much lagged behind the average growth of the country as a whole so that we find disparities in the per capita income between this whole region including Bihar, in particular, and the rest of the country, have widened and the disparity between the state average and the all-India average has continued to increase over a period of time.

This region, the whole of the eastern zone, is full of potentialities. In fact, if there is any region in the country where the difference between the actual achievement and potential is the largest, it is the eastern zone including Bihar. This only points to the potential for development and appropriate strategies have to be found out. The poverty ratio or the proportion of population living below the poverty line is also among the highest in this region. Therefore, the index of development as well as of poverty in the country as a whole reflects the progress that has taken place in this region. Unless the rate of growth of economy is accelerated in this region, i.e., the whole of eastern zone, and unless there is a significant reduction in poverty in this region, we cannot say that the country as a whole has made progress or we have been able to reduce poverty in the country.

If we look at the performance of Bihar in the Plan period, one should be happy to note that after all in the case of agricultural performance and rural development, the state has not been lagging behind the all-India average. I am not speaking of per capita income; per capita income in Bihar is the lowest in the country. But the rate of growth has not been the lowest, particularly if we take the agricultural performance, although it is still low. This only suggests that the response of the people to innovations and to investments is positive and encouraging. For instance, we can see the performance of wheat. The area under wheat has increased and so has the output. This only shows that the farmers here have responded very favourably to the introduction of new technology. The labourer in Bihar is as hard-working as any labourer in any other part of the country. In fact, one may even say that because of poverty, they are even more hard working than their counterparts in many other parts of the country. I have seen Bihar's labour in very far-off places and even in hilly areas as far as Himachal Pradesh and many other places. I saw them working there very hard at very low wage. In fact, I stopped at several places to discuss, to argue with them, to find out from them where they came from and what is their original profession and what is their wage. There is no doubt that potential-wise, this region is very promising and in terms of the efforts and responses also, it is promising.

But there are several historical factors which really explain why Bihar, in particular, and the whole of eastern zone, in general, have continued to remain backward. I think, many people who are interested in studying the regional disparities in development, take 15th August 1947, or 1951 when the First Five Year Plan was started, as a benchmark. I think, it is not very reasonable. It is meaningful in a certain limited sense. But in trying to understand the backwardness and the factors that account for the backwardness and development, one will have to go deeper in history. It is important to understand the historical background of these regions in relation to other regions of the country in order to understand the causes of backwardness and also in order to formulate the future strategy of development as well as to mobilise the resources from the rest of the country for the development of the region. I think the economic history of this country, particularly of this region suggests that during the century and half before Independence, the rate of taxation was very high in the whole of the eastern zone and the extraction of surplus from rural sector was much higher, whether you take it per capita or per hectare, than in many other parts of the country. Of course, we all know that there had been a significant drain of resources from this country in the colonial period. But there is no doubt that there was also a significant interregional flow of resources. There are regions wherein the investments made in the infrastructure like transport and irrigation in the pre-Independence period was much higher than the resources mobilised within that region and certainly eastern zone was not one of the regions where investment was made significantly in that period. In fact, it is held by several economic historians, that in the whole of the colonial period this region was neglected with regard to public investments. I would not hesitate in asserting that in the whole of century and half before Independence, there was a significant outflow of resources from the whole of eastern belt which was partly frittered away in conspicuous consumption and partly invested in other regions. Now, development is not merely a question of resources. After all, this extraction of surpluses from the whole of this zone under the permanent settlement system was associated with the growth of a set of institutions, the land tenure system and the whole set-up which was very different from the Ryotwari system or Mahalwari system which were conducive to development. The whole region has inherited a very poor resource base in terms of infrastructure.

This was accentuated by population pressure in the last 30 years after Independence. And over and above this, the transfer of resources from the rest of the country to this region was not significant at least upto the end of Third Plan period. I have figures which show that per capita transfer of resources to Bihar and to some of the states of this region was lower than the all-India average upto the Third Plan period whether it is an account of Finance Commission's transfer or Planning Commission's transfer. But then, in the recent period, the transfer of resources per capita is higher than the all-India average. It can be said that the per capita transfer according to Finance Commission award and from Planning Commission according to Gadgil Formula, are now higher than the all-India average. But in spite of higher per capita transfer, the per capita plan outlay in this region is much lower than investments in some of the developed states and it is also lower than the all-India average, because the per capita plan investment is determined not only by the resources transferred according to Planning Commission formula, but also the surpluses that state itself has over the non-plan expenditure. The surpluses are lower because of lower per capita tax which itself is due to lower per capita income. The tax mobilisation or the resource mobilisation depends on taxable capacity in general and taxable capacity is determined by the per capita income and also by the level of urbanisation, and how the income is distributed and several other factors.

I am not suggesting that the transfers which are being made now either according to Gadgil Formula from Planning Commission or according to the Finance Commission formula are optimal. I am not suggesting that there is no scope for improvement. In fact, I have no hesitation to say that there is a scope for greater progression in both the cases but that will not solve the problem because, as I have suggested, ultimately it is own per capita surplus which becomes important, and among several other factors, per capita surpluses are determined by the flow of private investments also. When we talk of plan of development, we have in mind not only the public investment but also the private investment, and as the Chief Minister rightly pointed out, there is an outflow of financial resources from the state through the financial institutions. The credit-deposit ratio is lower here than what it ought to have been. So again, the infrastructure that has been built up in the pre-Independence period in some of the states still has its impact on the mobilisation of resources in those states from the private sector. The industrially developed states because of their better infrastructure, because of their better institutional background which means managerial ability etc., and the whole tradition of industrial development, have been able to attract more from the financial institutions from all over the country. Therefore, this is also a factor to be taken into account from the point of view of planning, development and policy. It becomes extremely important to attract more resources from private investment and to induce the financial institutions to invest more in the region. Thus, there has to be a concerted effort to mobilise the resources not only on account of federal transfer but also on account of the saving within the region and private investments, in general.

As I mentioned earlier, the very factors which explain why the per capita income is lower and the per capita revenue is lower, are also the factors which reveal that the institutional framework and the tradition has not been conducive to rapid economic growth. I had the occassion to study some 10 years ago the land tenure relations in certain parts of Bihar and I still remember I went back with the feeling that there was greater scope for redistribution of land in certain parts of Bihar. Anti-poverty programmes require some land base. The landlessness in this state is very high. Therefore, the programme for poverty removal requires a greater land base.

If you want to support the poor through a livestock programme by giving animals, it cannot be successful until some land is there for fodder production. Similar is the problem in encouraging poultry programmes. Here again, land is required. Homestead programmes also require some land. Therefore, in a situation like Bihar there needs to be a greater effort for acquiring more land for the purposes of poverty removal.

And then because of the same tradition, which I have mentioned, there needs to be a greater governmental effort apart from the involvement of voluntary organisations etc. In fact, nobody will dispute the proposition that people's participation has to be increased. If we have to make our planning effort a success, village *panchayats* and voluntary organisations have to be involved. But there is no doubt, that again as compared to some of the developed states, we do not have large number of people who can contribute voluntary efforts and skills. Thus, the role of the government in bringing about change is more important in this region than in many other states.

Our education system is already lopsided. We have a structure whereby we are adding more of knowledge and skills at higher levels and at a very low rate at the bottom levels. In the context of under-development or backwardness, if we want to bring about rapid change both through population control as well as through the pursuit of viable economic activities, the literacy level becomes very important particularly for girls. Literacy level in Bihar is certainly among the lowest in the country. And this means, of course, investment and whenever there is crisis of resources and the revision of plans, it is the social services which are drastically cut down all over the country, not only in Bihar. But in this particular part of the country, we need to tone up the literacy level, the primary education becomes extremely important. All of us have been fortunate enough to get higher education for long years and have necessary expertise in various ways to help improve literacy at the lower level.

So where land is scarce, the capital resources are scarce, the role of labour and educated persons becomes extremely important. Certainly, we are abundant in labour resources. This is one of the few resources of our country where the potential for utilisation still exists. If you want to get the maximum out of the scarce capital resources and the scarce managerial resources, the mobilisation of our labour resources and the administration and even the educated personnel becomes extremely important. So far as the labour is concerned, this means better organisation and better work discipline, so that we produce more per unit of time from our power plants or from our several public sector enterprises. The university education which has been fairly widespread luckily in Bihar as in many other parts of the country provides, I think, the best sources of voluntary effort in trying to solve the problems of the people. I would like to suggest that the uiversities and the colleges should adopt certain villages for certain programmes and the government should be willing to cooperate in this involvement of propagating certain new ideas and in organising the poorer people in their effort to improve their standard of living. I think, the time has come when we need to move into rural areas to experiment with development programmes in the villages and to interact with the people and find out what are the practical difficulties and problems so that even intellectually our tools get sharpened and ideas get clarified.

Keynote address at the National Seminar on *Planning for Development and Removal of Regional Imbalances with Special Reference to Bihar* held at L.N. Mishra Institute of Economic Development and Social Change, Patna, September 29-30, 1982.

3 | Development of Tribal Areas

The Case of Bastar

The problems of remote tribal areas characterised by long distances and insufficient accessibility are well-known. But it would be useful to reiterate some of them, especially the order of priority that needs to be accorded to the solution of these problems.

The most glaring problem is a vacuum in administration caused by a large number of unfilled vacancies at various levels of development administration and the lack of adequate motivation and the requisite competence among those present. The problems of the area are so challenging that only those officers who are properly motivated, competent and possess a very high integrity would be able to contribute to the development process and ensure justice to the tribal population. In fact, there is a widespread feeling that, in general, only those officers who are not particularly known either for their competence or integrity are sent to this district—a place where these qualities are needed most. Such postings amidst numerous vacant positions in an otherwise difficult and exploitative environment can have undesirable consequences. I, therefore, feel that a special effort is needed to institutionalise the selection of properly motivated and competent officers to work in this area with the definite prospects of new postings elsewhere after a specified period of tenure and with due recognition of work done by them towards the development of such backward areas. Such a personnel policy would not involve any investments, to begin with. It only requires a switch-over to a new personnel policy and procedures. To sustain such a personnel policy over a long period would, of course, require substantial investments in the provision of residential quarters, reasonably good schools for the children of the officers, adequate number of vehicles for the officers to reach the villages etc. I have returned from this visit very much reinforced in my conviction that both the Finance Commission and the Planning

Commission need to give special attention to the requirements of upgradation of administration in such areas as the cost of provision of services is considerably high because of inaccessibility and long distances.

Another parallel measure needed for the personnel policy is the training of the local people, especially the young literate tribals, in various skills and professions and to absorb them in various positions within the district. Apart from obviating the need to bring a large number of people from outside by overcoming various constraints, such a policy would provide a dependable mechanism for ventilating the felt needs of the tribals and for minimising their exploitation. These two measures, namely, bringing good officers from outside and training up the local people for various postings, would fill up the large vacuum that appears to exist now in the sphere of development administration and would thus help to bring the people closer to the administration by bridging the communication gap. I returned with a feeling that this vacuum in administration and the communication gap is largely responsible for whatever encouragement that the extremists get for their activities in this area.

The restructuring of the administrative set-up on the above lines, is an essential prerequisite for implementing effectively the measures for the development of the area and for the betterment of the tribals. On the basis of my impressions gathered during this visit, I would like to suggest the following measures in a rough order of their importance:

1. There seems to be a case for raising the prices fixed by the government for the minor forest produce. The producer's share in the consumer's price appears to be very low at present. This could be raised; but it would be equally important to ensure that the benefits accrue to the primary sellers and not to the middlemen. This can be ensured only if the administration and people are brought closer to each other.

2. The minimum wages already fixed by the government need to be ensured in practice. This again would be possible only if a closer and effective monitoring is done by the administration. The initiative of the tribals, especially the young and the literate among them, needs to be raised for this purpose. In general, it would be possible to enforce minimum wages in those activities where people are

required to work in large clusters, easily amenable to the surveillance by the administration.

3. There is an immediate need for extending primary health services, especially in remote areas like Abhujmad area. The infant mortality rate in this area seems to be very high due to the incidence of malaria as well as severe malnutrition. It is even suspected that the tribal population has remained stationary in the last few decades due to high infant mortality. I was told and myself discovered in a few places even in the Abhujmad area that tribals are, by and large, receptive to modern health services. The local youth trained in some of the skills concerning health services, would be particularly helpful.

4. The institution of *ashram* schools is going to be by far the most important instrument for bringing about growth as well as social justice in tribal areas in the long run. I need not dwell on the various merits of this system. The contents of curricula at these schools also deserve some scrutiny so as to make them more relevant to the problems of the area.

5. There is a widespread demand for handpumps for drinking water. Its impact on the health of the population, both by saving labour and prevention of disease, is immense. The repair services for the pumps already installed are also important. Again, the local youth can be trained to undertake such jobs.

6. Public distribution of essential commodities like salt, cloth and kerosene on an extensive scale would have considerable impact on the welfare as well as productive efficiency of the tribal population. The *ashram* schools can become centres for such a distribution system so as to minimise pilferage.

7. Development of irrigation, wherever possible, especially through lift irrigation, can raise the yield per acre of rice substantially. The low rice yields prevailing at present are a principal cause of nutritional deficiency.

8. There is a great need for constructing new roads, especially the approach roads. In several places, I found that the tribal population is willing to contribute labour voluntarily as *shramdan* towards such

construction. The prospects of mobilising labour for productive activities like irrigation and roads, seems to be much greater in tribal areas like Bastar where people are traditionally used to community effort under local leadership for gainful purposes.

9. It is necessary to straighten the records of landholdings by undertaking fresh surveys wherever necessary. This is especially necessary for Abhujmad area where no such records seem to exist. Without the proper records of individual ownership rights on land, it would be difficult to ensure the flow of institutional credit for supporting various farm development and anti-poverty programmes.

December 31, 1982 when the author was Member, Planning Commission.

4 Growing Regional Disparities in Development in India

Post-Reform Experience and Challenges Ahead

It is now well established that the inter-state disparities in the growth of GSDP have increased in the post-economic reform period beginning from the early nineties when compared to the eighties. In general, the richer states have grown faster than the poorer states (Ahluwalia, 2000; Dev and Ravi, 2003; Bhattacharya and Sakthivel, 2004). The regional disparities in per capita GSDP growth are even greater because the poorer states in general have experienced a faster growth in population.

Although these disparities have accentuated in the post-reform period, they have been building up in the pre-reform period itself. For example, in the early 1960s the per capita GSDP of the richer states like Punjab, Maharashtra and Gujarat was, on an average, about 80 per cent higher than the average per capita SDP of the bottom four states *viz.*, Bihar, Uttar Pradesh, Orissa and Madhya Pradesh. This disparity increased to 125 per cent by the early 1970s (Rao, 2005); was contained at a little over 100 per cent during the eighties; and escalated steeply to 200 per cent towards the end of the nineties.

States whose per capita GSDP is below the national average together account for over 60 per cent of the country's population and as high as 75 per cent of the country's population below the poverty line. Further, these states account for nearly 60 per cent of the population belonging to the socio-economically disadvantaged sections like scheduled castes (SCs) and scheduled tribes (STs). There is thus a large potential for growth which needs to be exploited for sustaining development in the country over a long

I am indebted to G.R. Reddy, C. Ravi and N. Sreedevi for their help in the preparation of this paper.

period. This is necessary for improving regional and social equity and for strengthening national integration.

Sectoral Composition of Growth

How does one explain the accentuation in inter-state disparities in development in the post-reform period in the country and, indeed, the tendency of a gradual build-up in these disparities over the plan period? One way to study is to decompose by looking at the emerging regional disparities with respect to the individual sectors, i.e., the primary, the secondary and the tertiary. The inter-state variation in per capita GSDP originating from the primary sector, measured by the coefficient of variation, has always been lower than that from the secondary sector GSDP. There is also no evidence of an increase in its variability across regions in the post-reform period when compared to the eighties. This is understandable because agriculture is based essentially on land and labour which are widely distributed across the country. There are, no doubt, significant regional disparities in the availability of physical and institutional infrastructure for agriculture like irrigation, rural electricity and institutional credit. However, despite these constraints, technological changes in Indian agriculture represented by the Green Revolution were adopted widely in the country, including especially the eastern region, by the end of the eighties.

The GSDP per capita from the secondary sector, on the other hand, shows much higher variability across regions and this variability rose significantly in the post-reform period. The tertiary sector which has been the prime mover of GDP growth in the post-reform period has generally grown faster in the industrially advanced states and shows a significant rise in its variability across states during this period. We know that there has been a steep reduction in the share of the primary sector in the overall GDP, a modest rise in that of the secondary sector and a big rise in the share of the tertiary sector. Thus, the decline in the relative importance of the primary sector—which shows lower disparities—and the rise in the importance of the other two sectors showing higher variability explain, at the compositional level, the rise in inter-state disparities in per capita GSDP in the post-reform period.

Whereas inter-state disparities in per capita GSDP have increased significantly in the post-reform period, the corresponding disparity in human development index (HDI) has declined. The coefficient of variation in HDI declined from 22.6 in 1981 to 19.0 in 1991 and 16.3 in 2001. This is because investment requirements in primary education and primary health care are not as heavy as in the capital-intensive physical infrastructure, and the results in terms of improving literacy rate and the life expectancy at birth are relatively quick. However, the rise in public expenditure in these sectors has been very slow, especially in the poorer states, in the post-reform period (Dev and Mooij, 2003). This is reflected in the smaller decline in regional disparities in HDI in the post-reform decade. Since human development has a positive impact on GDP growth, inadequate attention to this sector in the poorer states in the post-reform period could also be responsible for the rise in regional disparities in per capita GSDP.

Causal Factors

Investment

Planning and Public Investment

Investment in physical and human capital, technical change and institutions, including those of governance, are the three key variables usually invoked for understanding the growth performance. A glaring feature of the investment scene in the post-reform period is the steady decline in the rate of public investment and a steep rise in the share of private investment with a stagnation in the rate of total investment. According to the estimates by the Central Statistical Organisation, gross capital formation by the public and private sectors were roughly equal at around 10 per cent of GDP each in the early 1980s. Public sector investment declined to a little over 7 per cent of GDP in recent years whereas private sector investment rose significantly.

The decline in public investment is even more glaring at the state level where bulk of the public expenditure on irrigation, power and social sectors is incurred. This is indicated by the fact that the share of the states declined from around 50 per cent of total plan expenditure in the country in the eighties to 40 per cent towards the close of the nineties.

Within the states, the per capita plan outlays of the poorer states have always been much lower than those of the better-off states. These disparities have widened in the post-reform period. For instance, during the Sixth Plan period (1980-1985), the actual per capita plan expenditure for the poorest four states, on an average, was a little over half of the average per capita plan expenditure of the better-off states like Gujarat, Maharashtra and Punjab. But during the Ninth Plan period (1997-2002), this proportion came down to around 40 per cent.

Central assistance for state plans (including assistance for externally aided projects), which is a major component of state plan resources, has been progressive in that the per capita assistance for the poorer states has been higher than for the richer states. The poorer states have been handicapped basically by their own weaker resource position. The per capita own plan resources of the poorer states, including market borrowing, constituted around 40 per cent of own per capita plan resources of some of the better-off states, *viz.*, Punjab, Maharashtra, Haryana and Kerala during the Sixth Plan period. This ratio deteriorated to 28 per cent in 2003-04 and further to less than 20 per cent in 2004-05. An important factor responsible for this deterioration in the financial position of the poorer states is the decline in the tax-GDP ratio of the Centre in the post-reform period and the consequent decline in the transfers to the states through devolution as recommended by the Finance Commissions. The loss to the states, that is, the difference between the devolution estimated by the Finance Commissions and the actual devolution, amounts to Rs. 100,000 crore for the decade 1995 to 2005 (Reddy, 2005). The decline in per capita transfers to the poorer states was even greater because the formula for devolution by the Finance Commissions is quite progressive. Therefore, the 12th Finance Commission has done well by raising the tax devolution by 1 percentage point (Government of India, 2004).

As expected, among states, there is a strong positive correlation between the per capita income and tax-GDP ratio. For richer states, because of their higher tax-GDP ratio, their own tax revenues per capita are much higher than those for the poorer states. This is so even when the tax effort of some of the richer states is lower, and that of some of the poorer states higher than the desirable norm considering their per capita income, rate of urbanisation, etc. Although the tax devolution by the Finance

Commissions has been progressive for the last 25 years, this could not offset the weaker resource position of the poorer states so far as resources for plan are concerned. Higher tax devolutions from the Finance Commissions have helped them basically to reduce their dependence on grants-in-aid for meeting their deficits on non-plan revenue account. In the absence of progressive devolution of tax revenue, the Finance Commissions would have had to take greater recourse to grants-in-aid for filling up the non-plan revenue gaps of such states. However, it must be said to the credit of the 12th Finance Commission that they have raised the proportion of grants in the total devolution and earmarked a significant portion of these grants to the poorer states for the development of social sectors like education and health.

The debt-GDP ratios of the poorer states are higher. Because of their lower creditworthiness they have not been able to access borrowings from the market to the same extent as the richer states. The per capita market borrowings of the four poorest states which were almost equal to the market borrowings of certain better-off states, *viz.*, Punjab, Maharashtra, Haryana and Kerala during the Sixth Five Year Plan declined to 72 per cent of such borrowings by these states in 2004-05. The inability of the less developed states to access sufficient resources for the development of infrastructure through higher plan outlays has thus emerged as a critical constraint in redressing regional imbalances in development.

Among states, the correlation between per capita GSDP growth rate in the post-reform period of nineties and the index of social and economic infrastructure in 1995 as well as 2000 is positive and significant. Clearly, the states whose initial or pre-reform conditions were favourable in respect of infrastructure could benefit more from the opportunities opened up, especially in the service sector, by economic reforms and register higher growth rates in GSDP (Rao and Dev, 2003).

Private Investment

This is because private investment has been flowing basically to the high income states where per capita plan outlays have been higher and where, therefore, infrastructure is well developed. For example, according to the IDBI data, the per capita cumulative disbursements by the all-India financial institutions up to March 2004, were Rs. 15 lakh for Maharashtra,

14 lakh for Gujarat and 7 lakh for Tamil Nadu, as against less than 3 lakh for Madhya Pradesh, less than 2 lakh for Uttar Pradesh, and less than half a lakh for Bihar. Similarly, in 2003, investment plus credit-deposit ratios of scheduled commercial banks were high for the western (75%) and southern regions (79%) and quite low for the eastern (54%) and central regions (50%). As to the amount of FDI (foreign direct investment) and FTC (foreign technical collaboration) approved from August 1991 to December 2000, a few advanced states, *viz.*, Maharashtra, Gujarat, Tamil Nadu, Karnataka and Delhi together accounted for half the share as against the combined share of less than 10 per cent by the four poorest states (Government of India, 2001).

Technical Change

The issue of technical change does not seem to figure prominently in the debate on regional disparities in development in India. This could be partly because much of the technology is embodied in capital equipment and hence is highly correlated with such investment. Also, this may be attributed to the speedy diffusion of frontier technologies like biotechnology and information technology across regions and even among income groups with large differences in asset endowments, when adequate support services are provided. The success of green revolution in India provides a classic illustration of this process. After the initial success with wheat in the north-western India for a decade beginning from the mid-sixties, it soon spread to different parts of the country by the eighties covering rice even in the poorer eastern Gangetic plains because of its inherent profitability and relatively low investment requirements.

The experience so far with information technology is equally encouraging and holds the prospect for raising productivity enormously in millions of farms and factories of varying sizes and the government offices throughout the country. This experience underlines the need to exploit the potential offered by these emerging technologies as well as human development for giving a fillip to the catching-up process in the less developed areas of the country.

Institutions and Governance

Historically, the developed states are, in general, characterised by progressive land tenures like the Ryotwari or the Mahalwari systems, whereas most of the less developed states were under the exploitative tenures like the Zamindari and the Jagirdari systems. Many of these areas were under the princely states for a long period. The social structure evolved under progressive land tenures has been conducive to the growth of enterprise and generated incentives for work, whereas the social structure perpetuated by the exploitative land tenures has been inimical to enterprise and bred apathy. Also, historically, the developed states have had relatively more efficient systems of governance in terms of skills, responsiveness and the quality of delivery systems. Unlike capital—which is highly mobile across regions and continents—good governance cannot be transplanted in an area, as it evolves basically within the prevailing socio-political structure over a long period. An outmoded social structure can never bring about or sustain good governance in the modern sense. On the contrary, it can frustrate exogenous attempts at good governance by its debilitating and corrupting influence.

The current debate on 'good governance' in India is largely divorced from the nature of the prevailing social structure and the need to generate socio-economic impulses for its transformation. As such, it comes out essentially with technocratic prescriptions regarding good governance in the poorer states as a prerequisite for attracting greater investment flows and for stepping up growth through the efficient use of resources. It underplays the role of factors like investment in infrastructure, technical change for raising the profitability of investment and empowerment of the people in triggering off the desirable changes in the prevailing socio-economic structure, which is the root cause of poor governance and inefficient delivery systems in the less developed areas.

For understanding the causes of backwardness and for formulating appropriate development strategies, one has to go deeper into the history. For example, for over a century and half before Independence, the rate of taxation was very high in the eastern zone and the extraction of surplus was much higher than in many other parts of the country. We know that there has been a significant drain of resources from the country in the colonial period. But there was also a significant interregional flow of resources within the country. There was a large net outflow of resources from the eastern region which was partly frittered away in conspicuous consumption and partly invested in other regions in infrastructure like irrigation and transport (Rao, 2005). This is how the less developed regions inherited poor infrastructure and outmoded institutions at the time of independence.

Even after Independence, the per capita transfer of resources from the Finance Commission as well as the Planning Commission were lower for many of the less developed states for at lest two decades when the cost of building infrastructure was relatively low (Rao, 2005). The transfer of resources, especially from the Finance Commissions, have become progressive after the seventies. But in a federal democratic polity there are limits to such statutory transfers, particularly because many of our 'developed' states too are poor in absolute terms.

The Way Ahead

It is clear from the foregoing discussion that for reducing regional disparities in development, improving social and economic infrastructure in the backward regions through greater public investment needs to be given the highest priority in the development strategy. The other two areas of priority action for these regions are: speeding up social transformation through the empowerment of the common people and measures for good governance. In this presentation, I have chosen to focus mainly on the inter-state disparities in levels of development. However, growing regional disparities within certain states, especially the bigger ones, is a matter of equal concern. It is clear from the development experience and the simmering unrest in several less developed parts of the country that without major initiatives at the national level, the regional disparities in development may accentuate further to crisis proportions threatening social harmony and national integrity, apart from depriving the nation of the opportunities for higher and sustainable development.

Unfortunately, precisely at this moment when imaginative and decisive initiatives are needed towards this end by the Centre, there are conflicting signals emanating from the policy-making levels, and a clear and coherent policy is yet to emerge. The 12th Finance Commission, while linking the debt write-off scheme for states with the quantum of reduction in their revenue deficits, fixed norms, targets and the time-frame that are uniform across all states regardless of their initial levels of revenue deficit, income levels and debt-GSDP ratios. The permissible level of fiscal deficit under the Fiscal Responsibility and Budget Management Act is uniform across all states. Further, the recommendation of the 12th Finance Commission to dispense with the loan component of Central assistance for state plans and leaving the states to directly access the market for loans can adversely affect the development of the poorer states whose creditworthiness is lower, unless, as suggested by the Finance Commission, the Centre volunteers to intermediate on behalf of the poorer states. Therefore, an alternative framework for enabling the poorer states to step up their developmental expenditure needs to be quickly put in place by the Planning Commission.

The Mid-Term Appraisal of the Tenth Five Year Plan, by the Planning Commission, recognises the growing regional disparities, and states that "the objective of bringing about greater regional balance must be the overriding consideration for determining the use of Central funds that flow as Central assistance to State Plans" (Government of India, 2005: 512). The Commission notes the inadequacy of the existing pattern of central assistance for state plans, through the Gadgil Formula, for making progress towards mitigating these imbalances and suggests that, "The actual flow of funds to backward areas resulting from the operation of the Formula till date needs to be analysed and the Formula may need to be revisited in the present day context" (p.508). But with the acceptance of the recommendation of the 12th Finance Commission to dispense with the loan component of plan assistance, there is not much left for revisiting, except the grant component! At the same time, the Commission expresses helplessness in modifying the Formula and gives up any hope when it says that, "the recent proposals for modification have not been able to generate the required consensus among states. It appears that the normal Central assistance is likely to continue in its present form in the near term" (p.512).

Such constraints notwithstanding, there is a strong case for renewing efforts at revising the Gadgil Formula, if only for making the grants component of Plan assistance more favourable to the less developed states.

This is especially necessary if the quantum of grants is to be raised substantially to help such states in view of the constraints in accessing loans in the market. It is indeed ironical that Central assistance for state plans, whose avowed purpose is to ensure speedy development of the poorer states, is less progressive than the devolution from the Finance Commissions. This is because the latter has been left to be decided by a few experts whereas in the case of the former, consensus among states is indispensable (Vithal and Sastry, 2002).

Even so, before making their recommendations, the Finance Commissions have been holding extensive discussions with state governments as well as with various sections of our population. It speaks highly of the trust that our people have reposed in the constitutional arrangements of our federal democratic polity that the recommendations of the Finance Commissions have been received, by and large, favourably. This suggests that a far-sighted leadership can still generate consensus among states and people at large on the need for a more progressive formula for Central assistance for state plans in the interests of preserving social harmony and strengthening national integration.

The predominant weight now given to population (60%) in the Gadgil Formula needs to be brought down substantially to the level assigned in the Finance Commission formula (25%), which has become acceptable. The latest figures of population should be used for the distribution of this amount among states. The existing practice of using 1971 population is iniquitous as it penalises populous states for their lower level of socio-economic development—arising from their weaker resource position—which is indeed the basic cause for their high population growth (Rao, 2005).

Certain criteria presently used, *viz.*, tax effort, fiscal management, population control, female literacy, on-time completion of externally aided projects and success in land reforms—which together claim 7.5 per cent of resources for distribution—need to be revisited. For one thing, the measures of 'tax effort' and 'fiscal management' currently used, being different from those used by the Finance Commissions, are far from satisfactory. Besides, the contribution of allocations, based on these criteria, towards fulfilling the avowed objectives is dubious. This is because several other factors are far more important in improving the indicators chosen. They are also iniquitous because the allocations on the basis of these criteria benefit mainly the better-off states who, in any case, have the requisite resources for improving these indicators. The amount saved by modifying or dispensing with the above criteria (42.5%) may be distributed among states on progressive criteria like the deviation and the distance methods, as used now under the Gadgil Formula for the distribution of 25 per cent of Central assistance.

While mediating on behalf of the poorer states to access market loans, Centre should ensure that the resultant resources for plan are distinctly more progressive than hitherto under the existing formula. Unlike the Tenth Plan's original proposals, the Mid-Term Appraisal does not seem to favour rigidly linking Central assistance with the implementation of reform packages or other measures concerning good governance. It may, nevertheless, be desirable to put in place mechanisms for ensuring that the additional resources so accessed are in fact utilised for the development of social and economic infrastructure.

The Mid-Term Appraisal also projects several proposals to strengthen the resource position of the backward states, such as raising the royalty for the poorer states which are rich in forests and minerals; helping them through better project preparation etc., for accessing the Additional Central Assistance for the Externally Aided Projects; Backward Regions Grants Fund (BRGF) to address regional balance concerns; and refocusing Bharat Nirman project for rural infrastructure development as well as central sector expenditure from various ministries for the development of the poorer states.

At the end, it is heartening to note that the Planning Commission would like to "see itself in a more proactive role in championing the cause of states with the Central ministries in key policy issues that have strong equity and regional balance dimensions. In a liberalised, market-driven policy environment, the responsibility of the Commission is greater in that it has to ensure a level playing field for less developed states and regions" (Government of India, 2005: 513).

References

Ahluwalia, Montek S. (2000). "Economic Performance of States in Post-Reform Period", *Economic and Political Weekly*, 6 May.

Bhattacharya, B.B. and S. Sakthivel (2004). "Regional Growth and Disparity in India: Comparison of Pre- and Post-Reform Decades", *Economic and Political Weekly* 29(10), 6 March.

Dev, S.M. and Jos Mooij (2003). "Patterns in Social Sector Expenditure: Pre- and Post-Reform Period", (*mimeo*). Hyderabad: Centre for Economic and Social Studies.

Dev, S.M. and C. Ravi (2003). "Macroeconomic Scene: Performance and Policies', in C.H.H. Rao and S. Mahendra Dev (eds.), *Andhra Pradesh Development: Economic Reforms and Challenges Ahead*. Hyderabad: Centre for Economic and Social Studies.

Government of India (2005). *Mid-Term Appraisal of 10th Five Year Plan*. Planning Commission.

Government of India (2001). *Handbook of Industrial Policy and Statistics*. Department of Industrial Policy and Promotion.

Government of India (2004). *Report of the Twelfth Finance Commission (2005-10)*.

Rao, C.H.H. (2005). *Essays on Development Strategy, Regional Disparities and Centre-State Financial Relations in India*. New Delhi: Academic Foundation.

Rao, C.H.H. and S. Mahendra Dev (2003). "Economic Reforms and Challenges Ahead: An Overview" in C.H.H. Rao and S. Mahendra Dev (eds.), *Andhra Pradesh Development: Economic Reforms and Challenges Ahead*. Hyderabad: Centre for Economic and Social Studies.

Reddy, G.R. (2005). "Twelfth Finance Commission and Backward States". (*mimeo*). Hyderabad: Centre for Economic and Social Studies.

Singh, Ajit Kumar (2005). "Finance Commissions Devolutions and Regional Imbalances", paper presented at the National Seminar on *Accelerated Economic Growth and Regional Balance –Recent Experiences and Implications for Inter-State Variations in Development*, organised by the Indian Economic Association, Institute for Studies in Industrial Development and Institute for Human Development, New Delhi, September 16-18.

Vithal, B.P.R. and M.L. Sastry (2002). The *Gadgil Formula for Allocation of Central Assistance to State Plans*. Hyderabad: Centre for Economic and Social Studies.

Lecture dedicated to the memory of Prof. A.M. Khusro, at The 88th Annual Conference of The Indian Economic Association, December 27-29, 2005, organised by School of Economics, Andhra University, Visakhapatanam, Andhra Pradesh, published in the *Indian Economic Journal* 54(1), April-June, 2006.

Section II

Smaller States

5 Rationale for Smaller States
The New Imperatives

The consolidation of imperial power was the overriding consideration behind the organisation of states under British rule in India. The goals of imperial power required that a province be composed of heterogeneous groups with respect to language, culture and the levels of socio-economic development. However, this strategy failed to split the people on emotional grounds because of the common bond provided by the national movement for Independence. Nevertheless, British policy resulted in marked regional differences with regard to the levels of economic development and the cultural patterns even between the people speaking the same language. This is because, in many cases, people speaking the same language were split and brought separately under the jurisdiction of different provinces and the princely states. Centuries of separation have thus fostered sub-regional patterns even among the people speaking the same language.

When the reorganisation of the states was undertaken in independent India in the mid-fifties, linguistic homogeneity became the main consideration. This is understandable because the Indian National Congress countered the British strategy by declaring as its objective the reorganisation of states on a linguistic basis and by constituting its provincial units on this pattern. Moreover, there was a phenomenal growth of regional languages in the process of the revival of national consciousness. Linguistic homogeneity, therefore, emerged as a primary factor for the reorganisation of states immediately after Independence. It was too early for the goals of independent India to find their expression on the question of reorganisation.

More than two decades of planned economic development under the democratic system has given rise to a set of forces which could not be foreseen earlier. These forces are the direct result of the pursuit of economic development within the states which had inherited marked regional unevenness.

In the first place, the growth of the public sector entailed major decisions in regard to the allocation of resources within each state. As can be expected, the politically dominant region or the one with a majority vote in the state gained at the expense of the minority region. Politically dominant regions need not be economically developed, although in a large majority of cases the dominant regions happen to be relatively developed. Since even the so-called developed regions in India are underdeveloped in the absolute sense, there would be a resistance to the diversion of resources in a significant way from the relatively developed to the underdeveloped regions within the state.

Secondly, government has become the major source of employment. The secondary and the university education have grown since Independence out of all proportion to the growth of the economy, thus giving rise to the problem of educated unemployment. The politically dominant region within a state can appropriate to itself a larger share of jobs than it is entitled to on the basis of its population. The problem becomes acute when the minority region happens to be economically backward.

Thirdly, political dominance implies the denial of political power to the minority region. In a democracy, political participation gets identified, to a large extent, with the sharing of power at various levels, and the denial of this power to the leaders of the minority region can give rise to frustration and tensions.

Thus, the inherited sub-regional patterns within some of the existing states have led to the 'unequal' distribution of investible resources, jobs and political power. Where the dominant region happens to be underdeveloped, this unequal distribution may appear to be equitous. In either case, however, the unequal distribution leads to regional tensions within the states. Economic development within a democratic set-up requires the willing participation of the people in an environment of peace and stability. Therefore, the disquieting feature of the existing set-up is the emergence of regional tensions.

These regional tensions could probably be avoided or at least postponed for a fairly long period even within the existing framework of states if progressive and dynamic policies are pursued for a rapid expansion of employment opportunities. Policies such as land reforms and those for the redistribution of income and wealth, if effectively implemented, can give a new orientation to the peoples' expectations by offering opportunities for development which outweigh the possible regional gains and losses. Such policies could also curb the 'vested interests' who seek to exploit the regional sentiments for their own ends.

Experience has demonstrated the failure of the progressive forces to give a radically new direction and purpose. Nor is there any prospect of such a thing happening in the near future. Under these circumstances, the recurring regional tensions within the states are becoming a fertile ground for the 'vested interests' to pursue their own ends by disrupting the unity of the people and by making it difficult for the governments to pursue even the moderate tasks of economic development. This results in the weakening of whatever progressive movement that exists.

It appears that states constituted on a homogeneous basis free from the sense of regional domination would be more conducive to the growth of progressive forces, as the people will then be able to see more clearly the lasting solutions to the problem of poverty and unempoyment. They can be expected to show more initiative, drive and confidence as is clear from the experience of Punjab and Haryana after the states were separated.

It is important to note the main characteristics of the emerging regional movements for separate statehood. As argued above, these forces are the consequence of economic growth in the post-Independence period within a framework of states constituted on the basis of the ideals espoused in the pre-Independence period. These forces should, therefore, be regarded as reflecting the growing maturity of our system and indicating the need for a better organisation for growth.

One of the most important characteristics of these emerging forces is their spontaneity. There was a time when even a moderate political movement required a strong and highly motivated leadership. But the present separatist agitations are unprecedented because the people themselves are launching them on their own initiative and are attracting political leadership to their side. The 'vested interests' are volunteering their help only at a later stage when the movements concerned have already been initiated by the large, organised and vocal classes comprising NGOs, students, teachers, engineers, lawyers and physicians.

To understand these trends, it is necessary to bear in mind the increasing role of government or public investments and the crucial significance of education and skills in economic growth. It is true that these urban middle classes constitute a small proportion of the total population but the rural people in general are found actively sympathising with such movements partly because a large section of the present-day urban middle classes hails from the countryside and also because agriculture has been neglected in certain regions.

Another interesting feature of some movements is their secular character. For the first time in the recent period one finds rational economic considerations dominating over those of language, religion and caste. For instance, the agitators for a separate Telangana include, apart from the Telugu speaking people of the region, persons who speak Urdu, Hindi, Marathi, Kannada, Tamil, Gujarati and several other Indian languages. Even people from the Andhra region who settled down in Telangana before the formation of Andhra Pradesh are active in this agitation. Similarly, Reddis, Kammas, Brahmins and Harijans are active in the separatist movements both in the Andhra and the Telangana regions. Therefore, the sooner we grasp the nature of the emerging forces the better it would be for the balanced growth of the country on secular and democratic lines.

Regional affinity as expressed in the will of the people should be made the basis for the reorganisation of states. This may involve linguistic homogeneity not in the sense of 'one language—one state' but in the sense of a large majority of the people in such homogeneous regions speaking the same language. Such regions are also likely to be homogeneous in terms of their economic characteristics, and may have the same historical background. The point to note is that when the will of the people is made the basis, it is most likely to be crystallised around a region which is homogeneous with respect to the above characteristics. We have worked our institutions long enough to be able to objectively ascertain the wishes of the people in various ways.

The rapid growth of population in the last two decades and the enormous growth of public responsibilities and functions have caused an undue strain on the administration of some of the larger states. In some of these states one does not find regional unrest or tensions. It is possible that this apparent cohesion is due to the slow economic growth in these states which itself might be traceable, among other things, to the largeness of their size. Fortunately, there are no strong feelings for the integrity of large states. There would, therefore, be little resistance to the reorganisation of these states if such a course is considered desirable.

Apart from administrative efficiency, there are at least two strong considerations in favour of breaking up some of these large states into smaller ones. First, a large state will have a large volume of investible resources at its command even if the per capita resources are smaller than the national average. The sheer size of these resources can enable such states to concentrate on particular regions through lumpy investments. This may, in course of time, lead to regional imbalances and political tensions. Secondly, a larger state can exercise undue influence at the Centre both in the acquisition of resources as well as in shaping the power structure at the Centre. Smaller states in a federal framework may legitimately resent such an undue influence exercised by a few units.

One of the arguments advanced in favour of larger states is that they ensure financial viability. A situation where a larger state composed of two distinct economic regions is considered necessary for financial viability implies that the surplus from one region compensates for the deficit of the other. This very fact, if it persists over a long period, may lead to regional tensions within the state and would thus undermine the solidarity of the people. Another argument advanced is that a larger state would be in a better position to undertake infrastructural investments requiring a large amount of resources. But, as pointed out earlier, the politically dominant regions may derive proportionately larger benefits from such investments which could also become a source of regional tensions.

Experience has shown, however, that the infrastructural investments by the states have fallen below the expectations. This is due partly to the heavy dependence of the states on the Centre for resources under the existing financial arrangements and partly to the inter-state disputes such as those relating to the river valley projects. These considerations suggest that some of these infrastructural investments, particularly those which benefit more than one state, be undertaken by the Centre. Indeed, such a takeover by the Centre would become imperative when the states become smaller in size.

So far, in practice, it has been difficult to ensure an equitable allocation of resources as between the regions within a large state. It would, however, be easier for the Centre to allocate more resources in per capita terms directly to the backward (smaller) states. A redistribution of resources from the rich to the poor regions (states) via the Centre is a more feasible proposition than such a reallocation within the larger state.

Past experience indicates that the states with per capita income below the national average received, in general, more central assistance in per capita terms than the other states. The per capita incidence of taxation, on the other hand, bears a proportionate relationship to the per capita income of states. These facts implied a redistribution of resources from the richer to the poorer states via the Centre. However, one cannot be sure of the same process of redistribution between the developed and the backward region within the states. Available evidence suggests that the regional disparities within the states might have increased during the Plan period.

It is also argued that private capital from the prosperous regions can flow more easily into the less developed ones within the large composite states. This argument has no logical basis. Nor is it borne out by experience. The present regional conflicts relate essentially to the distribution of benefits from the public investments and public employment. This is to be expected because investment creates employment and as such, this would be welcome whether it comes from the public or the private sectors. One can indeed expect a growing competition between different states for attracting private capital. The migration of private capital and skills across the states in India is a well-known phenomenon. To take an instance, the area under the Nizamsagar Project in Telangana witnessed large scale migration of progressive farmers from coastal Andhra much before the Andhra and the Telangana regions were integrated into one state. Such private enterprise has remained unaffected by the separatist disturbances.

Yet another argument advanced against the constitution of smaller states is that the 'unproductive' expenditure on the administration would increase. It is true that the national per capita expenditure on administration may rise somewhat in the first instance as the number of states increases. But the productivity of such expenditure may also increase in smaller states. Lower per capita expenditure in a large state might prove to be uneconomical if the results are not encouraging. What is relevant, therefore, is not the absolute expenditure but the results per unit of expenditure incurred.

There has been a tendency for the employment under the government to increase at a rapid rate, a good part of which cannot be rationally explained but can only be regarded as a response of the system to the growing unemployment. To a certain extent, therefore, the increase in administrative expenditure and the additional empolyment in the newly created states should be regarded as a substitute for the expenditure that would have to be incurred anyway within the existing larger states.

The resistance to the reorganisation of states comes not merely from the considerations mentioned above but also from the fear of loss of power by the party bosses at the Centre if their home states become smaller. This explains the persistent refusal of a certain section of the Central leadership to see the realities even when it is common knowledge that some of these separatist movements are unprecedented in their intensity and scale. There has been an unfortunate tendency to treat such movements as a 'law and order' problem instead of displaying understanding and imagination with a view to restructuring our federal organisation.

It is true that the division of some of the existing states might open up a series of issues such as the division of assets and liabilities, the location of capital in the case of some of the newly formed states and the distribution of water of the common rivers. These could prove difficult to tackle and could well hold up progress in some of the newly created states if they are not sorted out in time. In many cases, the leaders of the regions concerned may volunteer to settle such disputes if the demand for reorganisation is genuine and widespread. The Centre should ask them to examine these issues thoroughly and come to an agreement before the states are reconstituted.

The best course for the reorganisation of states would be to approach each case on its merits. Any attempt at a once-for-all reorganisation of states all over the country on the basis of a fixed set of criteria is likely to be artificial and arbitrary and therefore unstable. This is because it would be difficult to expect public opinion to express itself clearly within a short period all over the country owing to its enormous regional diversity and unevenness. In any case, if there is openness of mind and flexibility on the part of the Central leadership, mistakes committed can be rectified in time and the wishes of the people when expressed can be given due consideration.

Seminar, April 1973.

6 | Uttarakhand: Need for Separate Statehood

[My acquaintance with Uttarakhand is over three decades old. I started visiting the hills as a tourist, but soon got interested in the developmental problems of the region. As a member of the Planning Commission between 1982-1986, I had the privilege of dealing with the subject of Hill Area Development. This provided opportunities for me to undertake extensive visits to this region and to study the problems on the spot by discussing with the people at the grassroots level. I have also had the good fortune of knowing, and interacting with, a galaxy of intellectuals, social activists, administrators and political figures hailing from Uttarakhand which provided opportunities for me to understand the problems of the region. Moreover, during the summer of 1988, when I was heading the Advisory Council on the Implementation of 20-Point Programme, constituted by the then Prime Minister late Shri Rajiv Gandhi, I had an opportunity to spend nearly a month in the remote areas of Pithoragarh district and discuss the problems of implementation of rural development programmes with the villagers as well as the officials at the local level. Their feeling of neglect was evident from the repeated expression of surprise, though delightful, over my presence in their midst in this remote area which, according to them, very few either from Delhi or Lucknow cared to visit! While it is distressing to see widespread unemployment and poverty amidst natural beauty, one cannot but be moved by their simplicity, truthfulness and honesty, who are also highly God-fearing (or God-loving?)!]

The current agitation for the formation of a separate state of Uttarakhand has been triggered off by the move to introduce reservation in jobs on the basis of the principle of 'uniformity' within a state. Superficially speaking, this agitation for separate statehood would appear to be a means to get over the reservation issue. But fundamentally, this represents a protest against the refusal to recognise the special features of the hill region and the disabilities it suffers from. It is a protest against the prevailing practice of administering the hill region through remote control by applying 'uniform' yardsticks throughout the state despite the great regional diversity in this large state. The hill areas of Uttar Pradesh continued to remain backward with meagre opportunities for livelihood on account of defective development strategy and ineffective implementation of schemes. This is a consequence of a 'straitjacket' approach inherent in a large state. But for these reasons, the agitation for the formation of Uttarakhand would not have assumed such serious proportions. Therefore, this agitation is neither accidental nor unexpected. Indeed, if there was no objective basis for separate statehood, the agitation would have been focused on the percentage of reservations in jobs as such. This is what has been happening in several other states. In fact, the people of Uttarakhand deserve to be complimented for quickly extricating themselves from internal dissentions and channelling their movement in a forward-looking direction.

At the intellectual and the planning level, the problems of the region have been well understood. The difficult topography of the region, the accentuation of hardships following the snapping of the traditional trade links with Tibet, the unsuitability of the soils for cultivating field crops, the increasing denudation of forests due largely to commercial felling to satisfy the rising demand from the plains, the incentive for educating children as the only alternative source of earning, the large out-migration of able-bodied males and the consequent emergence of 'money order economy' with increasing feminisation and senilisation of the hill economy and society, etc., have been well documented. It is also recognised that the hill areas have a comparative advantage in horticulture and agro-processing which have a favourable export demand besides being environment-friendly; that the expansion of public distribution of food grains is necessary to protect the environment by discouraging the cultivation of food crops; and that there is a great potential for the location of pollution-free industries which are skill-intensive such as electronics and the related software. The need for the active involvement of the people, particularly women, for the protection of environment has been repeatedly stressed. It is also well recognised that the women power, the resources of disciplined and trained, but unemployed, ex-army personnel, and the skills of educated youth remain to be harnessed. What is more, there is a separate department of Hill Area Development which is entrusted with the task of planning and implementation of the development programmes for the region by channelling funds including special assistance from the Centre for the purpose.

Despite all this, if the impact in terms of development, conservation of environment and the expansion of employment opportunities has not been satisfactory, and if the feeling of neglect persists in the region, the inescapable conclusion is that all this wisdom has largely remained on paper and has not been backed by effective administrative arrangements for putting these ideas into practice. It is readily acknowledged that there is no regional planning worth the name for the hill areas in Uttar Pradesh. The so-called regional plan is reduced essentially to putting together of schemes undertaken by various departments at the state capital; at best 'regional planning' amounts to monitoring of resources into the region on account of such schemes. The rural development programmes, for example, are still formulated and implemented according to the rigid guidelines issued from the state capital, despite the conditions in hills being vastly different from the plains. To give another telling example, despite the fact that women undertake the major responsibility for agricultural operations, and despite the repeated assertions that the latent power of women would be harnessed, there is hardly any woman extension worker or *gramsevika* in place in the remote areas, with the result that the extension workers usually while away their time with unemployed men in tea shops without transmitting any knowledge to the women farmers in the field!

The basic explanation for the failure to formulate and implement effectively the regionally relevant plan is simply that the power to formulate and implement such a plan is not vested in the region itself. The administration of a large state composed of diverse regions suffers from its irrelevance as well as ineffectiveness. On account of the irrelevance of its policy approach to any specific region, its ineffectiveness becomes a blessing in disguise to some extent, as the harm inflicted could be greater when wrong policies are implemented effectively! In practice, however, irrelevance itself is often responsible for ineffective implementation, apart from inaccessibility of services inherent in a large state. Historically, our states in most cases were organised in the colonial period on considerations which suited the rulers at that time. Speedy development of a region was certainly not one such consideration. After Independence, states have been reorganised from time to time on linguistic and other considerations in response to agitations by the people concerned. Development as such was rarely the guiding principle, although the small size of some of the states resulting from reorganisation has proved to be conducive to their speedy development. Punjab, Haryana and Himachal Pradesh are clear examples of this. In smaller states, the ministers and the civil servants have an intimate knowledge of each village and the people in turn can easily approach the powers that be when need arises. The relative homogeneity of the state ensures the relevance of the development plans formulated; and smaller distances and fewer number of people ensure the accessibility of services and effective implementation of schemes.

Despite the protracted debate in the country on the need for decentralised planning at the district and village levels, decentralisation in planning in India is effective today basically at the level of states *vis-a-vis* the Centre. At this level, decentralisation does seem to have promoted growth, and where institutional reforms have been successful, it seems to have made a favourable impact on social justice also. The effectiveness of planning at the state level depends very much on the size of the state. The smaller the size of the state, the greater is its ability to take decisions quickly, to design programmes in response to the felt needs of the people as well as in keeping with the resource endowments of the region, and to implement them effectively. The size of the state, its relative homogeneity and the structural changes brought about seem to have had a greater impact on growth and social justice so far than formal decentralisation of planning below the state level.

In the big states like Uttar Pradesh, Bihar, Madhya Pradesh and Rajasthan, decentralisation of planning at the sub-state levels is highlighted as a felt need and one finds a visible concern among politicians and administrators for decentralised planning. However, it is precisely in these states that decentralised planning is least successful. It appears as if the very largeness of size which necessitates decentralisation militates against it. For one thing, a larger state is also, as a rule, a more powerful unit in terms of concentration of political as well as bureaucratic power. Devolution of functions and resources to a large number of districts, or even at sub-regional level, would mean immediate parting with enormous power enjoyed by the politicians and bureaucracy at present as also foregoing opportunities for the distribution of patronage. Secondly, decentralisation within a large state involves considerable amount of effort at the state level by way of coordinating and monitoring developmental work relating to innumerable units. These states are thus too large and centralised to embark upon decentralisation.

It is, however, wrong to believe that regardless of the size of the state, decentralised planning at the district level, when it is effective, can go a long way in reducing regional disparities in development. For one thing, the backwardness of each of these regions, consisting of a number of districts, arises either from specific agro-climatic factors or from long periods of neglect before they were merged into composite states. What is required, therefore, to tackle the backwardness of these reigons is an integrated approach to the planning of infrastructure for each of them. This is necessary even for making district planning effective by providing infrastructure which is beyond the district-level outlays. The potential district-level Plan outlays account for only about 25 to 30 per cent of state Plan outlays. This means as much as 70 to 75 per cent of outlay is still planned and allocated at the state level for various infrastructural items including, particularly, power and major and medium irrigation, which have a bearing on the development of the individual districts. Besides, in a mixed economy like ours, the level and pattern of private investment, particularly in the non-agricultural sectors, which can be influenced by state policies, is an important determinant of development.

The larger states, especially those composed of highly heterogeneous units, have failed to reduce disparities in development between different regions. Marathwada and Vidarbha in Maharashtra, Saurashtra and Kutch in Gujarat, Telangana and Rayalaseema in Andhra Pradesh, and Uttarakhand in Uttar Pradesh are clear examples. When some of these areas were merged to constitute the linguistic states at the time of states' reorganisation, as in the case of Maharashtra and Andhra Pradesh, despite the recommendation to the contrary by the States Reorganisation Commission, it was done with the assurance that special steps would be undertaken to bring these backward regions on par with the developed regions. However, the politics of planning in a democratic set-up within the state as a political unit have been such that it became increasingly difficult to impose sacrifices on the developed regions to benefit the backward regions. The evidence, on the contrary, points to the accentuation of disparities as in the case of Marathwada, Vidarbha, Rayalaseema and Uttarakhand. This has happened despite the constitutional provisions to safeguard the interests of the backward regions through the establishment of Regional Development Boards with special powers to the Governors for monitoring the progress, as in the case of Maharashtra and Gujarat.

The size and the relative homogeneity of the state as a unit of governance assume special significance in the country in the context of the ongoing economic reforms. The basic philosophy underlying these reforms for sructural adjustment is to promote efficient utilisation of resources by releasing the creative energies of entrepreneurs and the people at large. This is to be done by opening up the economy and encouraging competition with a view to providing incentives for technological upgradation and innovation. It is also recognised that for these reforms to be compatible with social justice, the state has to play an important role towards empowering the common people by enlarging their freedoms, widening economic opportunities for them and improving their skills and capabilities.

The state governments have started competing with each other for attracting capital and technology from outside by offering various incentives. They have to take steps to improve their delivery systems for reaching the targeted poor so as to provide basic social services efficiently. All this requires 'good governance' for promoting development with social justice. Already, the indications are that the smaller and efficient states, especially those infrastructurally well-placed, are better able to attract capital and entrepreneurship. As expected, among the bigger states, such resources are moving into regions which are better endowed with infrastructure. If the state governments fail to improve infrastructure in the backward regions and fail to improve social services in general for the weaker sections, then the accentuation of regional disparities and income inequalities is almost a certainty. Since the role of the state has become important to speedily cope with the adverse consequences of structural adjustment, and indeed for influencing such adjustment in a direction that is humane and equitable, 'good governance' has to be put on the top of the agenda for reform. A situation is fast developing when the existing organisation of at least some of the big states may become incompatible with the objective of economic reforms, i.e., stepping up efficient and equitable growth.

In the new context, when efficiency of resource-use and equitable development have become the prime objectives, viability of a state defined as a relatively homogeneous administrative unit rather than its 'financial viability' should be the overriding consideration in organising the state boundaries. Basically, the idea is that even if the amount of resources which are being allocated presently for a backward region in a composite state remain the same after reorganisation, the content of plan as well as the quality of its implementation would improve vastly to justify such reorganisation. As it is, several big as well as small states are financially 'deficit', just as the 'surplus' states happen to belong to both the categories. Even though the degree or the severity of financial 'deficit' among states varies depending upon their natural endowments, historical background and levels of development, the fact remains that even some of the biggest states in the country, whose per capita income is among the lowest, show deficits even after the devolution by the Finance Commission. Many of the smaller hill states today depend almost entirely on central assistance for their state plans.

So far as Uttarakhand is concerned, even though it is part of a larger state, the accepted practice for long has been to provide special central assistance in order to ensure that its plan outlay is comparable to that for Himachal Pradesh. For example, during the Seventh Plan, special central assistance accounted for nearly 60 per cent of the plan outlay for Uttarakhand, as against over 80 per cent in the case of Himachal Pradesh. Under the existing system of federal financial transfers in India, both by the Finance Commission and the Planning Commission, certain objective and rational criteria have been evolved over a period of time, through a process of consensus-building, which take into account the own capacity of a state to mobilise resources as well as its legitimate needs. Whereas financial resources are thus transferable on the basis of rational criteria, political will and administrative capabilities, which are essential prerequisites for the efficient use of resources, are not so transferable!

It is unfortunate that even in a democratic polity like ours, political consensus in the region seeking separate statehood, and even consensus at the level of the composite state concerned, have failed to persuade the Centre to accede to the demand. States have often been reorganised in the past only in response to protracted and violent agitations. In the case of Uttarakhand, the state legislature has unanimously passed resolutions twice in favour of separate statehood under two different sets of governments. Let us hope that imaginative, forward-looking and development-oriented approach to reorganisation of states would prevail and procedures would be evolved to resolve such issues through peaceful and democratic means by ascertaining the consensus as well as through expert examination by a high-level independent body. But the formation of Uttarakhand need no longer be delayed, because both political consensus and expert opinion are overwhelmingly in its favour.

Mainstream, Annual Number, 1997.

Section III

Statehood for Telangana

7 | **Budgetary Surpluses
of Telangana**

There have been complaints that the Telangana region has not got its due share in the public expenditure of Andhra Pradesh state ever since its formation in 1956. At the request of the State Chief Minister in January 1969 for an independent investigation, the Comptroller and Auditor General of India deputed K. Lalit, an officer of the rank of Accountant General, for determining the exact quantum of Telangana surpluses for the period from 1-11-1956 to 31-3-1968. These surpluses (or the difference between the amount that ought to have been spent and the amount actually spent for Telangana) were to be computed on the basis of the principles agreed to by all the political leaders on January 19, 1969. Lalit submitted his Report in March 1969. Apart from his estimates of Telangana surpluses, Lalit's Report contains comprehensive data regarding annual receipts and disbursements under major heads for the 12-year period.

In the wake of widespread discontent in Telangana, the Government of India constituted a high-powered committee in April 1969, under the Chairmanship of Justice V. Bhargava, to determine the Telangana surpluses for the period from 1-11-1956 to 31-3-1968; to determine the sum which ought to have been spent on the development of the Telangana region but remained unspent on March 31, 1968; and to evolve and recommend precise principles for determining such surpluses in future.

Meanwhile, sharp differences of opinion have persisted between the Government of Andhra Pradesh and the Telangana Regional Committee (also called the Andhra Pradesh Regional Committee consisting of the members of Legislature from Telangana) concerning the criteria for the allocation of receipts and expenditure between the Telangana and Andhra regions. Neither the government nor the Telangana leaders scrupulously adhered to whatever understanding and agreements had been arrived at. The criteria have been revised frequently from both the sides.

This paper is primarily an attempt to examine these principles from the standpoint of an economist and to suggest a procedure for estimating Telangana surpluses. An attempt has also been made to estimate the magnitude of Telangana surpluses by using this procedure. The data used are those contained in Lalit's Report which has since been published by the Government of Andhra Pradesh.

We use the term 'Budgetary Surpluses' to include surpluses on revenue as well as capital account. These 'surpluses' should not be taken to mean amounts which have remained unspent in Andhra Pradesh and have been accumulated into reserves for the purposes of future developmental expenditure, for, no such accumulated reserves seem to exist in Andhra Pradesh now. Telangana surpluses are the amounts which ought to have been spent in Telangana but have been diverted for expenditure in the Andhra region. Therefore, these surpluses represent the difference between the due share of government expenditure for Telangana and the actual share. It is clear that such surpluses, if any, represent over-expenditure in the Andhra region.

Telangana Surpluses on Revenue Account

For estimating Telangana surpluses on the revenue account, we follow the principle laid down in the Gentlemen's Agreement of 1956 that "the balance of (revenue) income from Telangana should be reserved for the expenditure on the development of Telangana area". We use the figures of revenue receipts and expenditure given in Lalit's Report. This means that the procedure followed by the Government of Andhra Pradesh for allocating receipts and expenditure to the Andhra and Telangana regions remains unmodified. This procedure is open to criticism in certain respects. It is free from criticism in regard to many items which are specific to each region: Land revenue receipts and expenditure on schools or minor irrigation are among such heads. The difficulty arises in regard to the receipts accrued and expenditure incurred jointly for the state as a whole. For instance, the state's share in Union excise duties, grants-in-aid from Central government, etc., and the expenditure relating to general administration have been apportioned between the Andhra and Telangana regions in the 2:1 ratio. This is assumed to be the population ratio between the two regions and was affirmed time and again by the government as well as the Telangana leaders.

However, according to the 1961 Census the population of Telangana constituted 35.3 per cent of the state population[1] as against 33.3 per cent implied in the above ratio. The discrepancy of 2 percentage points in the allocation of receipts and expenditure over a period of 12 years can make a significant difference to the magnitude of surplus or deficit. This will become clear later in this paper. The apportionment of capital expenditure on 2:1 (66.7:33.3) basis yields a deficit of Rs. 14 crore for Telangana whereas apportionment on the basis of actual population (i.e. 64.7:35.3) turns this deficit into a surplus of about Rs. 3 crore. The use of 2:1 ratio is, therefore, inequitous, especially because nearly 80 to 90 per cent of revenues accruing from the Central divisible pool and other Union taxes are distributed among the states strictly on the basis of population.

However, we had to use the figures as they are because there is no way of identifying from the available data all the heads, especially in regard to expenditure, which have been apportioned on the 2:1 basis. There is no doubt, however, that a reallocation of receipts and expenditure on the basis of population is called for in the interests of equity. Our estimate of revenue surplus would thus be subject to revision on this account.

A major point of controversy in regard to the allocation of receipts relates to the grants-in-aid from Central government under Article 275 of the Constitution. Lalit has argued that, "successive finance commissions had recommended the payment of grants to State Governments to cover revenue gaps. Strictly speaking, the amounts received from the Government of India under this head insofar as statutory grants are concerned should be allocated between the two regions, on the proportionate overall revenue gap existing between the two regions..."[2] However, Lalit followed the prevailing practice of apportioning these grants on 2:1 basis in view of the agreement to this effect between the Chief Minister and the Chairman of the Telangana Regional Committee. But the

---

1. Bureau of Economics and Statistics, Government of Andhra Pradesh, *Handbook of Statistics, Andhra Pradesh, 1966-67*, p.17.

2. K. Lalit, "Report on the Quantum of Telangana Surpluses", Government of Andhra Pradesh, p.17.

question as to how these grants-in-aid ought to be apportioned remains unresolved.

It is true that successive Finance Commissions have recommended these grants to states for meeting a substantial portion of deficits in their revenue budgets. The Third Finance Commission observed, for instance, that "the total amount of grants-in-aid should be of an order which would enable the States, along with any surplus out of the devolution, to cover 75 per cent of the revenue component of their plans".[3] Although Andhra Pradesh had a surplus of about 10 crore on revenue account over the 12-year period (see Table 7.3), it would show a significant deficit if we exclude grants-in-aid from revenue receipts. Therefore, a substantial portion of potential deficit has been covered by grants-in-aid.

However, these grants were intended to cover the anticipated deficits during the period of the Plan concerned and not the actual deficits incurred in the past. The anticipated deficits were worked out by the Finance Commissions largely on the basis of the projections of revenue and expenditure submitted by the state governments. The estimates of budgetary gaps were governed by a number of factors such as "the liability arising out of the changed pattern of Central assistance for post-stage II community development blocks...grants to universities...revision of pay scales in several States, reorganisation of police and district administration, introduction and extension of Panchayati Raj, continuance of subsidised sale of foodgrains, special relief measures, etc."[4]

In their memoranda to the successive Finance Commissions, the Government of Andhra Pradesh focused on the needs of the backward regions of the state. The following extracts bear this out:

"The poverty and helplessness of the *ryots* in these areas (Rayalaseema and Telangana) is appalling. Irrigation facilities are poor ... There are no major industries which could provide alternate employment for educated classes and labour in urban areas and the landless poor in the rural areas. Inadequacy of power supply is also coming in the way of development of small industries. Educational facilities, health services and communications are also very poor, particularly in the Telangana area...It is hoped that the Finance

3. Government of India (1961). "Report of the Finance Commission", pp. 31-32.
4. *Ibid*: 12.

Commission will make suitable recommendations for special financial assistance by way of additional grants-in-aid to the States which are backward in the fields of industrial development, education, health services, communications, etc... This Government requests that besides continuing the grant-in-aid of Rs. 4 crores per annum that is now being given by the Centre (under the Second Finance Commission Award) an additional grant-in-aid of at least Rs. 6 crores per annum may be recommended for the Third Plan period to cover at least a part of the anticipated deficit."[5]

It is thus clear that the state government requested for grants-in-aid in order to cover part of the anticipated deficit as a result of expenditures planned mostly for the development of backward regions. In practice, however, the expenditure pattern was such as to create a sizeable revenue deficit for the Andhra region and surplus for the Telangana region. Table 7.1 shows that whereas revenue receipts of Telangana (including one-third of grants-in-aid) constituted 41.7 per cent of state receipts, its revenue expenditure was only 36.8 per cent of state expenditure. Andhra region, on the other hand, showed a sizeable revenue deficit despite the fact that two-thirds of grants-in-aid are included in its revenue receipts. The distribution of grants-in-aid in proportion to the actual deficit is, therefore, unjust.

It may be argued that the areas whose per capita tax revenue is lower should be given preference for extending grants-in-aid, especially where the lower tax revenue is due to factors such as low per capita income or the introduction of prohibition. The Andhra region, one might argue, deserves consideration because prohibition was introduced in this area. The Third Finance Commission stated, for instance, that in determining the budgetary gap of each state, they had "taken full account of the impact of prohibition on the revenues of the states where this has already been introduced".[6]

It is, therefore, necessary to examine whether the grants-in-aid actually made to different states reveal any precise relationship with their per capita tax revenues. This is important because successive Finance Commissions regarded the tax effort of states as one of the basic considerations governing grants-in-aid. Summarising these principles, Asok

---

5. Government of Andhra Pradesh (1961). Memorandum Submitted to the Third Finance Commission, pp.24, 30-32.

6. Report of the Finance Commission, *op cit*: 12.

Table 7.1

Revenue Receipts and Expenditure of Andhra Pradesh

(Rs. crores)

Year	Receipts			Expenditure		
	Telangana	*Andhra Pradesh*	*Per cent of Col.1 to Col.2*	*Telangana*	*Andhra Pradesh*	*Per cent of Col.4 to Col.5*
	(1)	*(2)*	*(3)*	*(4)*	*(5)*	*(6)*
1956-57	10.94	25.44	43.0	6.45	22.98	28.1
1957-58	22.45	62.33	36.0	18.97	55.11	34.4
1958-59	26.67	67.52	39.5	22.43	63.42	35.4
1959-60	34.52	81.95	42.1	25.98	74.63	34.8
1960-61	33.52	85.28	39.3	30.00	84.98	35.3
1961-62	38.10	85.76	44.4	33.81	90.63	37.3
1962-63	45.07	105.34	42.8	38.38	100.80	38.1
1963-64	50.92	126.59	40.2	42.29	115.94	36.5
1964-65	53.76	131.57	40.9	47.65	127.13	37.5
1965-66	60.87	138.56	43.9	55.55	146.34	38.0
1966-67	70.44	157.25	44.8	63.76	169.67	37.6
1967-68	67.20	165.86	40.5	65.26	171.40	38.1
Total	**514.46**	**1233.45**	**41.7**	**450.53**	**1223.01**	**36.8**

Source: Lalit, K. (1969). "Report on the Quantum of Telangana Surpluses", Section IV, Government of Andhra Pradesh.

Chanda, the Chairman of the Third Finance Commission observes, "Liberal assistance to a State which had not used its taxing power adequately to narrow its budgetary gap would prove to be an inducement to it not to increase taxation. Secondly, it would benefit the more affluent tax-paying section of the population and not the poorer sections for whom federal assistance should obviously be granted."[7]

Table 7.2 gives a comparison of grants-in-aid to different states during the four-year period covered by the Second Finance Commission (i.e., from 1957-58 to 1960-61) with the state revenues (excluding grants-in-aid) and per capita income of the states. State revenues include the state's share in Central taxes, e.g., excise duties, income tax and estate duties. These

---

7. Chanda, Asok (1965). *Federalism in India—A Study of Union State Relations.* London: Allen and Unwin. pp.200-201.

revenues are distributed among states largely on the basis of population. Therefore, state-wise differences in per capita revenues (col.3 of Table 7.2) reflect the disparities in the mobilisation of revenues by the states. There is no systematic relationship between per capita grants-in-aid on the one hand and per capita state revenues or per capita income on the other. The analysis given in the Appendix shows virtually no correlation between them. In view of this experience, it would be difficult to argue that the Andhra region should be entitled to a larger per capita grants-in-aid than Telangana because of its low per capita revenues resulting from the

Table 7.2

Grants-in-Aid and State Revenues (Annual Average of the Four-year Period, 1957-58 to 1960-61, Covered by the Second Finance Commission)

(Rs. per capita)

State	Per Capita Grants-in-Aid	Per Capita State Revenues Excluding Grants-in-Aid	Per Capita Income 1960-61
(1)	(2)	(3)	(4)
Assam	9.06	19.08	333.34
Orissa	4.70	11.62	276.22
Mysore	4.70	25.31	304.71
West Bengal	4.02	19.93	464.62
All States	**3.67**	**18.05**	**334.54**
Rajasthan	3.40	14.98	267.43
Kerala	3.38	18.38	314.86
Andhra Pradesh	3.20	17.14	287.01
Madhya Pradesh	3.12	16.12	285.35
Bihar	2.89	11.00	220.69
Punjab	2.85	23.48	451.31
Tamil Nadu	2.77	20.01	334.09
Uttar Pradesh	1.87	14.99	297.35
Bombay	1.76	22.66	468.54*

Note: * The figure relates to Maharashtra.

Source: (1) Government of India (1961). "Report of the Finance Commission", pp. 101, 104-107.

(2) National Council of Applied Economic Research, "Distribution of National Income by States 1960-61", p.9.

introduction of prohibition. Nor can it be argued that the per capita grants-in-aid allocated to Telangana should have been larger because of its low per capita income. Population seems to be the only reasonable basis for apportioning grants-in-aid among the two regions. This procedure derives strength from the fact that among different states, there is a significant correlation between grants-in-aid and population (see Appendix).

Between different states, there is a significant positive correlation between per capita state revenues and per capita income. The statistical analysis shows that, on an average, an increase in per capita income by one rupee is associated with an increase of 4 paise in per capita tax revenues (see Appendix). In other words, a 1 per cent rise in per capita income is associated with 0.73 per cent increase in per capita tax revenues. If this all-India experience is taken as a norm, then per capita tax revenues of the Andhra region should have been higher than in Telangana because per capita income of Andhra is higher. If we assume that per capita income of the Andhra region is higher by 25 per cent when compared to that of Telangana (this is substantiated later), then the per capita tax revenues in Andhra should have been higher by 18.25 per cent (0.73 × 25).

Actually, however, the per capita tax revenue (excluding grants-in-aid) in Andhra for the 12-year period under study was Rs. 260 compared to Rs. 352.35 for Telangana, i.e., it was lower by 26 per cent. Ignoring the differences in per capita income, if Andhra had the same per capita revenue as Telangana, Andhra region would have mobilised Rs. 92 more per capita or Rs. 214 crore over 12 years. If we take into account the higher per capita income of Andhra and apply the all-India experience, the per capita tax revenue in Andhra should have been 18.25 per cent higher than in Telangana. This would have added another Rs. 148 crore bringing the total additional revenues to Rs. 362 crore.

There is no reason to believe that the tax revenues foregone in Andhra owing to the introduction of prohibition could not have been made good, at least in part, by other tax measures. Prohibition does not reduce the incomes of the people at large but only diverts the part of incomes either for savings or for expenditure on other goods and services. But assuming that the loss of revenues due to prohibition could not have been made good, what is the probable extent of loss on this account? The net revenue from excise duties in Telangana (after deducting revenue expenditure on this head) works out to Rs. 102.41 crore or Rs. 80.64 per capita for the 12 years. Assuming that excise duties would have yielded the same per capita revenues in Andhra, the total amount works out to Rs. 187.80 crore. If we deduct from this the actual excise revenues (net) in Andhra of about 5 crore, the probable extent of loss due to prohibition amounts to Rs. 182.80 crore.

It is clear from the above, that even when full allowance is made for the loss of revenue owing to prohibition and no adjustment in tax revenues is made for higher per capita income, it was possible to mobilise Rs. 31 crore (214–183) more in Andhra. If adjustment is made for higher per capita income and full allowance is made for the loss due to prohibition, about Rs. 179 crore (362–183) could have been mobilised from the Andhra region which is more than sufficient to cover its revenue deficit of Rs. 53 crore during the 12-year period.

The Telangana Regional Committee has been insisting ever since 1959 that "half of the overspent amount in Andhra revenue account should be added to the Telangana surpluses as the Government ought to have spent more in Telangana than its income."[8] At one stage, the state government also committed itself to this principle. In their letter to Lalit dated 28-2-1969, the government "clarified that the Telangana surpluses of each year should be computed by adding to the net revenue surpluses of Telangana region of that year half of the revenue deficit of Andhra area."[9] However, on second thoughts, the government clarified further on 6-3-1969 that "what was meant by revenue deficit in their letter of 28-2-1969 was that where capital receipts like loans from Government of India, etc., had been diverted to fill in the revenue gap of Andhra, half of the capital receipts so diverted should be added to the Telengana surpluses".[10] Consequently, Lalit decided to ignore the Andhra deficit altogether while computing Telangana surpluses on the ground that "it was not possible

---

8. Andhra Pradesh Regional Committee (1969). "Report of the Ad Hoc Committee on Planning on the Report given by Sri K. Lalit on the Quantum of Telangana Surpluses", (Report I), p. 7.

9. Lalit, *op cit.*: 5.

10. *Ibid.*

from the accounts to specify from what particular source the revenue deficit has been met".[11]

However, this question cannot be ignored as it has a direct bearing on the method of computing the net revenue surpluses of Telangana. Andhra Pradesh has a composite budget and the revenue surplus or deficit for the state as a whole represents the net position after the surplus or deficit of each of the two regions have been adjusted. Table 7.3 shows that during the 12-year period under study, Andhra Pradesh had a revenue surplus of Rs. 10.44 crore after adjusting the Andhra deficit (Rs. 53.49 crore) against the Telangana surplus (Rs. 63.93 crore). This implies that a good part of the Telangana revenue surplus has been diverted to Andhra for meeting its revenue deficit. The remaining part (Rs. 10.44 crore) being the revenue surplus of the state can be considered to have been diverted to the capital account of the state. Since a part of this amount has been spent for Telangana on capital account, adjustments needs to be made for this, before arriving at net Telangana surpluses on revenue account. For reasons discussed later in this paper, we are allocating 37.5 per cent of the capital expenditure of the state for Telangana instead of the prevailing practice of allocating 33.3 per cent. Therefore, 37.5 per cent of the revenue surplus of the state (i.e., 3.90 crore) will have to be deducted from the revenue surplus of Telangana (Rs. 63.93 crore) as estimated by Lalit, for arriving at the net revenue surplus (Rs. 60.03 crore).

This is the overall picture for 12 years. But what does this principle imply for the years when the state has a revenue deficit? Revenue deficit incurred for the state as a whole can be considered to have been covered by diverting the capital receipts or amounts from any other sources which could alternatively be used for expenditure on capital account. That is to say, revenue deficit of the state represents the expenditure sacrificed on capital account. Therefore, Telangana's share in the amount foregone (i.e., 37.5 per cent of the state's deficit) needs to be added to the revenue surplus of Telangana of that year for arriving at the net revenue surplus (see Table 7.3). Indeed, this appears to be the meaning of the suggestion contained in the government's letter to Lalit mentioned above.

---

11. *Ibid.*

Table 7.3

Telangana Surpluses on Revenue Account

(Rs. crore)

Year	Revenue Surplus (+)/Deficit (−)			37.5 Per cent of Col.3	Net Surplus (+)/Deficit (−): Col.2 - Col.4
	Andhra Pradesh	Telangana	Andhra Pradesh		
	(1)	(2)	(3)	(4)	(5)
1956-57	−2.03	+4.49	+2.46	+0.92	+3.57
1957-58	+3.74	+3.48	+7.22	+2.71	+0.77
1958-59	−0.14	+4.24	+4.10	+1.54	+2.70
1959-60	−1.22	+8.54	+7.32	+2.75	+5.79
1960-61	−3.22	+3.52	+0.30	+0.11	+3.41
1961-62	−9.16	+4.29	−4.87	−1.83	+6.12
1962-63	−2.15	+6.69	+4.54	+1.70	+4.99
1963-64	+2.02	+8.63	+10.65	+3.99	+4.64
1964-65	−1.67	+6.11	+4.44	+1.67	+4.44
1965-66	−13.10	+5.32	−7.78	−2.92	+8.24
1966-67	−19.10	+6.68	−12.42	−4.66	+11.34
1967-68	−7.48	+1.94	−5.54	−2.08	+4.02
Total	**−53.49**	**+63.93**	**+10.44**	**+3.90**	**+60.03**

Net revenue surpluses of Telangana thus worked out represent overspending in Andhra. This should be so unless the revenue surpluses of Telangana have been accumulated into reserves which are available for expenditure now. To the extent this amount is reimbursed from the future share of the Andhra region, the latter will cease to have the benefits of over-spending in the past. Therefore, the contention of the Telangana Regional Committee that half of the revenue deficit (or over-expenditure) of Andhra should be added to Telangana surpluses is unreasonable.

However, Telangana's claim would stand to reason if its surpluses are not reimbursed from the future share of Andhra but are met from the third source, say, Central government. But in such an event, it is not the half of Andhra deficit on revenue account alone that needs to be added to the Telangana surpluses. The aggregate of Telangana surpluses on revenue as well as capital account along with any interest that is agreed upon, would represent overspending in Andhra and, therefore, half of this amount should be added to Telangana surpluses, if the balance in public expenditure between the two regions is to be restored. If the correct population ratio for Telangana (35.3 per cent) is used, then the aggregate of surpluses should be raised by 54.5 per cent instead of 50 per cent only. The same procedure needs to be followed if Telangana surpluses are to be set aside from the receipts of the state first before apportioning the remaining receipts between the two regions. This is necessary, if the amount of Telangana surpluses is to remain the same as when it is set aside from Andhra's share of the state receipts.

Telangana Surpluses on Capital Account

Following the accord of January 19, 1969, mentioned earlier, Lalit worked out Telangana surpluses (or deficits) on capital account as the difference between one-third of the total capital expenditure of the state and the actual capital expenditure in Telangana. In the Gentlemen's Agreement of 1956, however, there was no reference to the ratio to be applied while allocating capital expenditure. The government and the Telangana leaders are agreed that capital receipts are not to be taken into account while calculating surpluses on this account, presumably because the bulk of the capital expenditure is met from loans and assistance from the Central government and overdrafts from the Reserve Bank.

Since the allocation of capital expenditure in the 2:1 ratio between the Andhra and the Telangana regions is based on the population ratio, it is only proper that the correct population ratio (64.7:35.3) is used, especially because the bulk of Plan assistance to states from the Central government is allocated on the basis of population. There is, for instance, a very high correlation between the population of the states and the Central assistance to them for the Third Plan. The inter-state variation in population explains as much as 86 per cent of variation in Plan assistance from the Centre for the Third Plan (see Appendix).

Apart from the population, economic backwardness of the region as indicated by its per capita income may be an important criterion for allocating capital expenditure. The ability of the region to mobilise its own resources has been regarded as yet another factor favouring more Central assistance. The Telangana Regional Committee has often pleaded for the distribution of Central assistance to the Andhra and Telangana regions in proportion to the own resources of these regions. But whereas the planners have been explicit on population and backwardness or per capita income as factors governing Central assistance, the position has by no means been straightforward in regard to the own resources of the states determining Plan assistance. The Third Five Year Plan clearly states that, "in assessing needs and problems, such factors as population, area, levels of income and expenditure, availability of certain services, e.g., roads, schools hospitals ... were taken into account".[12] On the question of own resources, however, the approach was flexible: "care was taken to see that States whose resources were unavoidably small did not have to limit development to a scale which was altogether insufficient, merely because of paucity of resources. At the same time States which were able to make a larger effort in mobilising their own resources could undertake development on an appropriate scale."[13]

Table 7.4 shows that among nine states whose per capita Central assistance for Third Plan was above the average (of all states), as many as eight states had per capita income below the average. Out of the six states with below average Central assistance, only two states have per capita incomes significantly below the average. The statistical analysis of these figures given in the Appendix shows that, on an average, a one rupee increase in per capita income is associated with a decline in per capita Central assistance to the extent of about seven paise. In other words, a one per cent increase in per capita income is associated with a 0.36 per cent decline in per capita Central assistance.

There is no positive correlation between per capita Central assistance and state's per capita contribution (see Appendix). On the other hand, there is a mild negative association between per capita Central assistance and per capita state's contribution. However, this may not imply that per capita Central assistance was lower because of higher per capita contribution of own resources. This relationship arises because per capita contribution is generally higher in states where per capita income is higher and higher per capita income is associated with lower per capita Central assistance.

------

12. Planning Commission, Government of India, Third Five Year Plan, p.60.

13. *Ibid.*

Table 7.4

*Central Assistance to States for Third Plan in Relation to States'
Contribution and Income*

(Rs. per capita)

State	Central Assistance	State's Contribution	State Income 1960-61
(1)	*(2)*	*(3)*	*(4)*
Jammu & Kashmir	171.60	0.73	289.02
Assam	84.23	27.27	333.34
Rajasthan	80.12	24.46	267.43
Orissa	77.82	49.73	276.22
Kerala	72.12	35.49	314.86
Madhya Pradesh	67.76	21.25	285.35
Mysore	66.46	40.00	304.71
Punjab	66.21	59.04	451.31
Andhra Pradesh	61.29	34.54	287.01
All States	**58.33**	**38.25**	**334.54**
Tamil Nadu	55.51	46.23	334.09
Gujarat	54.12	61.14	393.39
Uttar Pradesh	48.30	27.66	297.35
Bihar	46.47	24.94	220.69
West Bengal	44.36	41.57	464.62
Maharashtra	42.22	67.54	468.54

Source: (1) Government of India, Fourth Five Year Plan, 1969-1974, Draft, p. 75 (for cols. 2 and 3).

   (2) Government of India (1961). "Report of the Finance Commission", p.101 (for population figures).

   (3) National Council of Applied Economic Research, "Distribution of National Income by States, 1960-61" (for col.4) p.9.

A strong positive relationship exists between per capita income and own contribution of resources: A one per cent increase in per capita income of the state is associated with a 1.18 per cent increase in own contribution. In view of this experience the own contribution of the Andhra region can be regarded as poor when compared to Telangana's. The own resources of Telangana constituted 42.6 per cent of state resources for the Third Plan[14] (much higher than its population ratio of 35.3 per cent) despite its per capita income being lower than the Andhra region's. However, we are ignoring this factor in the allocation of capital expenditure between the two regions in view of the absence of any significant relationship between per capita contribution and Central assistance among states for the Third Plan. The experience of Central assistance to states discussed above strongly suggests the fairness of population and per capita income as the criteria for allocating capital expenditure between the Andhra and Telangana regions.

There are no separate estimates of per capita income for these regions. It is, however, possible to make a reasonable assumption as to the probable differences in the per capita incomes of these regions on the basis of the data on irrigation facilities, agricultural incomes and agricultural wages, etc.

Whereas Telangana accounted for 35.3 per cent of state's population and 41.8 per cent of state's area,[15] its share in irrigated acreage was only 27.9 per cent in 1965-66.[16] Thus, irrigated acreage per capita was higher in Andhra to the extent of 41.5 per cent when compared to that in Telangana. A study made by this writer in 1958-59 revealed the position as shown in Table 7.5 in regard to the net agricultural output and wages.[17] Even if equal weight is given to the Rayalaseema and the Delta regions, the net agricultural output per head works out to be Rs. 291.40 in the Andhra region or 100 per cent higher than in Telangana. The same holds true in regard to the wages of permanent labour while the wage rates of casual labour work out to be 34.4 per cent higher. Since agriculture is a major sector in the state contributing as much as 60 per cent to the state income,[18] it would be reasonable to assume that the per capita income of the Andhra region would be at least 25 per cent higher than that of Telangana.

---

14. Andhra Pradesh Regional Committee (1967). "Supplementary Report to the Tenth Report of the Subcommittee on Development on Implementation of Plan and Non-Plan Schemes in Telangana Area", p.4.

15. Bureau of Economics and Statistics, Government of Andhra Pradesh, *Handbook of Statistics, Andhra Pradesh, 1966-67*, pp.16-17.

16. *Ibid*: 60.

17. Hanumantha Rao, C.H. (1966). "Taxation of Agricultural Land in Andhra Pradesh", *Asia*, pp.41, 156.

18. *Handbook of Statistics, op cit.*: 10.

Table 7.5

Net Output Per Capita and Agricultural Wage Rates

(Figures in Rs.)

	Telangana	Rayalaseema	Delta
Annual Net Output Per Capita	146.56	103.26	479.45
Agricultural Wage Rates			
(i) Permanent Labour (per annum)	225.00	415.00	500.00
(ii) Casual Labour (per day)	0.93	1.25	1.25

If we apply the experience of Central assistance for state plans, *viz.*, a 1 per cent increase in per capita income should be associated with a 0.36 per cent decline in per capita Central assistance, the per capita assistance for the Andhra region should be 9 per cent (0.36 × 25) lower than for Telangana. By weighting the population ratio (35.3:64.7) with the ratio of per capita Central assistance (1:0.91), we get the allocation ratio between the two regions as 35.3:58.9. On this basis the shares of Telangana and Andhra regions in the capital expenditure of the state would be 37.5 per cent and 62.5 per cent respectively. Thus, the additional share for Telangana due to its low per capita income amounts to 2.2 per cent of state expenditure. In other words, the weight of per capita income in the allocation of capital expenditure for Telangana is about 6 per cent. This is considerably less than 10 per cent, proposed to be allocated to states on account of low per capita income during the Fourth Plan period.[19]

We have computed the Telangana surpluses on capital account as the difference been 37.5 per cent of state's capital expenditure and the actual capital expenditure for Telangana. The actual capital expenditure includes a few items, e.g., capital outlay on electricity schemes, payment of commuted value of pensions, floating debt and other loans and appropriation to the contingency fund, the expenditure on which is jointly incurred and has, therefore, been apportioned by the government on 2:1 basis between the Andhra and Telangana regions. We have reapportioned this expenditure on a 62.5:37.5 basis, because much of this joint expenditure may have to be borne in proportion to population. Failure to reapportion this expenditure

---

19. Planning Commission, Government of India, *Fourth Five Year Plan, 1969-1974*, Draft, p.53.

would result in an overestimation of Telangana surpluses. It is possible that there are a few more items of this nature requiring reapportionment. Insofar as the reapportionment ratio for Telangana (37.5 per cent) is higher than its population ratio, this may provide a corrective to the possible overestimation arising from our failure to account for some of these items. Needless to say, our estimate of surpluses would have to undergo revision if some more items of this nature are still left unidentified.

There may be certain other cases of reapportionment resulting in a clear upward revision of our estimate. For instance, the Telangana Regional Committee has argued that the existing allocation of the cost of Nagarjuna Sagar Dam on a 2:1 basis should be altered because the utilisation of water including the Krishna basin under this project would be in the ratio of 207:87 between the Andhra and Telangana regions. The Committee has suggested further that the expenditure on the Left Canal of this project should be shared between the Andhra and the Telangana regions in proportion to the actual benefits derived (44.4:87) instead of the present practice of allocating the entire expenditure to Telangana.

Lalit's method of allocating capital expenditure in the 2:1 ratio would show a deficit or over-expenditure for Telangana to the extent of Rs. 14.16 crore. If the correct population ratio (i.e., 35.3 per cent) is applied and the expenditure on joint items is reapportioned accordingly, then the actual capital expenditure on Telangana would be less than the desired expenditure yielding the surplus of Rs. 3.30 crore. If low per capita income of Telangana is also taken into account, i.e., if 37.5 per cent of capital expenditure is allocated to Telangana with corresponding reapportionment of expenditure on joint items, the Telangana surpluses on capital account would go up to Rs. 22.31 crore (see Table 7.6).

Telangana Surpluses on Account of Public Corporations

The All-Party Accord of January 19, 1969 laid down that "statutory or other boards, corporations, etc., functioning on a State-wide basis financed by the State Government would be, for the purpose of computing Telangana surpluses treated as if they were State-wide Government departments and as if their receipts and expenditure were booked in Government

Table 7.6

Telangana Surpluses on Capital Account

(Rs. crore)

Year	Capital Expenditure		37.5 Per cent of Col. 2	Surplus (+)/ Deficit (−): Col.3 - Col.1
	Telangana	*Andhra Pradesh*		
	(1)	*(2)*	*(3)*	*(4)*
1956-57	5.84	22.48	8.43	+2.59
1957-58	25.20	73.72	27.65	+2.45
1958-59	20.42	57.79	21.67	+1.25
1959-60	36.50	89.96	33.74	−2.76
1960-61	36.60	96.80	36.30	−0.30
1961-62	39.95	105.37	39.51	−0.44
1962-63	33.44	97.99	36.75	+3.31
1963-64	50.60	132.96	49.86	−0.74
1964-65	42.49	112.06	42.02	−0.47
1965-66	55.52	168.53	63.20	+7.68
1966-67	107.16	302.07	113.28	+6.12
1967-68	73.14	204.69	76.76	+3.62
Total	**526.86**	**1464.42**	**549.17**	**+22.31**

Source: Lalit, K. (1969). "Report on the Quantum of Telangana Surpluses", Section IV, Government of Andhra Pradesh.

accounts."[20] Lalit took into account only those corporations and boards, etc., in which the money invested by the state government formed 51 per cent or more of the share capital.

These corporations show a revenue deficit of Rs. 6.34 crore for Telangana over the 12-year period (Table 7.7). Lalit deducted this amount from the Telangana surpluses on revenue account for arriving at the overall surpluses. Lalit ignored the revenue deficit of these corporations in the Andhra region, just as he ignored the Andhra deficit on revenue account while calculating Telangana surpluses. Since Andhra Pradesh has a composite budget and since these corporations are to be treated "as if their receipts and expenditure were booked in Government accounts", it would be illogical to ignore the revenue deficit of corporations in the Andhra region. This is also unfair to Telangana because the Andhra region does not

---

20. Lalit, *op cit*: 3.

have revenue surpluses to meet the losses of public corporations. These losses in Andhra have to be met from other sources and Telangana should be entitled to meet its losses in a similar manner.

Table 7.7

Public Corporations—Telangana Surpluses on Revenue Account

(Rs. crore)

Year	Revenue Surplus (+)/Deficit (–)			37.5 Per cent of Col.3	Net Revenue Surplus (+)/ Deficit (–): Col.2-Col.4
	Andhra	*Telangana*	*Combined (1)+(2)*		
	(1)	*(2)*	*(3)*	*(4)*	*(5)*
1958-59	+0.03	+0.35	+0.38	+0.14	+0.21
1959-60	–1.00	+0.05	-0.95	–0.36	+0.41
1960-61	–1.11	–0.21	–1.32	–0.50	+0.29
1961-62	–1.47	–0.32	–1.79	–0.67	+0.35
1962-63	–2.80	–1.62	–4.42	–1.66	–0.04
1963-64	–1.02	–0.49	–1.51	–0.57	+0.08
1964-65	–1.31	–0.85	–2.16	–0.81	–0.04
1965-66	–2.74	–1.74	–4.48	–1.68	–0.06
1966-67	–4.05	–1.87	–5.92	–2.22	+0.35
1967-68	–0.58	+0.36	–0.22	–0.08	+0.44
Total	**–16.05**	**–6.34**	**–22.39**	**–8.41**	**+2.07**

Source: Lalit, K. (1969). "Report on the Quantum of Telangana Surpluses", Section IV. Government of Andhra Pradesh.

As argued earlier, any revenue deficit of Andhra Pradesh represents a draft on capital outlay and Telangana's share in this amount will have to be added to its surpluses (or deficit) for arriving at the overall surpluses. We, therefore, follow the same procedure now as we did in calculating Telangana surpluses on revenue account. Table 7.7 shows a surplus of Rs. 2.07 crore for Telangana on the revenue account of public corporations. This is because the losses in Andhra amount to more than its proportionate share of losses in the state.

Lalit worked out the Telangana surpluses (or deficits) on the capital account of these corporations as the difference between the actual capital outlay of these corporations in Telangana and one-third of the state's outlay. This procedure yields a deficit of Rs. 5.73 crore which he deducted from the Telangana surpluses on revenue account for arriving at the overall surpluses.

For reasons discussed earlier, we consider the desired capital outlay of these corporations in Telangana to be 37.5 per cent of state outlay instead of 33.3 per cent. Accordingly, we compute the Telangana surpluses on the capital account of these corporations as the difference between the 37.5 of capital outlay of these corporations and the actual outlay for Telangana. This estimate would be subject to revision because part of the capital outlay of these corporations represents joint investment and may have to be reapportioned according to the correct population ratio. While such a reallocation may lower our estimate, there may need to be some other reallocations which raise Telangana surpluses. For instance, the Telangana Regional Committee has been arguing with some justification that the original capital investment of the Road Transport Corporation whose activities were later extended to the Andhra region should be apportioned between the two regions and the "excess investment of Telangana should also be treated as Telangana surpluses".[21]

Table 7.8 shows that the actual capital outlay of public corporations in Telangana is less than the desired outlay by Rs. 1.42 crore which should be regarded as Telangana surplus on this account.

Present Value of Telangana Surpluses

The overall budgetary surpluses of Telangana, i.e., on revenue and capital accounts as well as on account of public corporations amount to Rs. 85.83 crore over the 12-year period. This figure of budgetary surpluses is an insufficient measure of the real value of economic loss for the Telangana region. The investment postponed implies the loss of several direct and indirect benefits in terms of income and employment and public revenues.[22] The Third Five Year Plan states that, "even a comparatively

21. Andhra Pradesh Regional Committee (1969). "Report of the Ad Hoc Committee on Planning on the Report Given by Sri Lalit on the Quantum of Telangana Surpluses" (Report I), p.5.

22. For a discussion of this aspect in relation to Telangana see Mathur, Gautam: "The Estimation of Telangana Development Fund", *The Graduate Monthly* II(8), Hyderabad. (This note was presented by Mathur to the Bhargava Committee on Telangana Surpluses.)

Table 7.8

Public Corporations—Telangana Surpluses on Capital Account

(Rs. Crore)

Year	Capital Expenditure		37.5 Per cent of Col. 2	Surplus (+)/ Deficit (–): Col. 3 - Col. 1
	Telangana	*Andhra Pradesh*		
	(1)	(2)	(3)	(4)
1958-59	0.66	1.50	0.56	–0.10
1959-60	2.00	6.67	2.50	+0.50
1960-61	2.76	7.71	2.89	+0.13
1961-62	4.67	10.59	3.97	–0.70
1962-63	4.43	10.17	3.81	–0.62
1963-64	5.72	15.95	5.98	+0.26
1964-65	8.41	24.53	9.20	+0.79
1965-66	12.04	34.60	12.98	+0.94
1966-67	12.95	33.66	12.62	–0.33
1967-68	9.33	26.34	9.88	+0.55
Total	**62.97**	**171.72**	**64.39**	**+1.42**

Source: Lalit, K. (1969). "Report on the Quantum of Telangana Surpluses", Section IV, Government of Andhra Pradesh.

small delay in completing a project and putting it into productive use can make a significant difference to the resources available for investment. The point is that as an economy develops, even marginal improvements in planning and execution over a number of points can yield a large return in the aggregate."[23] Owing to the steep rise in the general price index and in the construction costs during this period, the real value of the estimated surpluses has gone down significantly.

The real measure of loss from the investment foregone would be given by the social rate of return on investment which could be very high for our economy, say, 20 per cent.[24] However, we are suggesting a modest compensation by treating the Telangana surplus of each year as a loan for the Andhra region payable at a compound interest rate of 6 per cent per

---

23.   Government of India, *Third Five Year Plan*, p.116.

24.   Mathur, *op. cit.*

annum (see Table 7.9). The interest works out to Rs. 31.62 crore raising the overall Telangana surpluses to Rs. 117.45 crore.

Table 7.9

Overall Budgetary Surpluses of Telangana

(Rs. Crore)

Year	Overall Surpluses: as Computed in Tables 3, 6, 7 and 8	Interest at 6 Per cent Per Annum (compound) on Surpluses in Col.1	Cumulative Surplus with Interest
	(1)	*(2)*	*(3)*
1956-57	+6.16	0.37	6.53
1957-58	+3.22	0.59	10.34
1958-59	+4.06	0.86	15.26
1959-60	+3.94	1.15	20.35
1960-61	+3.53	1.43	25.31
1961-62	+5.33	1.84	32.48
1962-63	+7.72	2.41	42.61
1963-64	+4.24	2.81	49.66
1964-65	+4.72	3.26	57.64
1965-66	+16.80	4.47	78.91
1966-67	+17.48	5.78	102.17
1967-68	+8.63	6.65	117.45
Total	**+85.83**	**31.62**	**117.45**

Telangana Securities

Telangana inherited securities worth Rs. 13.59 crore as its share in the former Hyderabad state. The Government of Andhra Pradesh agreed to treat them as Telangana surpluses. The Telangana Regional Committee has demanded frequently that these securities be sold and the proceeds utilised for the development of Telangana. These securities are presumably intact and it may not be in the interests of Telangana to sell these securities until the surpluses or the overspent amount in Andhra is reimbursed and spent for the development of Telangana. These securities in Reserve Bank may prove to be highly beneficial for Telangana, in the long run, in terms of an easy access to much needed investible funds.

Conclusions

Our objective in this paper was not so much to give a 'precise' estimate of Telangana surpluses as to attempt a clarification of some of the main issues relevant to this problem and to suggest a procedure for estimating these surpluses. The limitations of data, especially those arising from the allocation of joint expenditures, will have to be overcome before the 'true' figure of surpluses can be arrived at. Our analysis suggests, however, that the Telangana surpluses could be sizeable. Even if 20 per cent margin of error is applied to our estimate, the surpluses would amount to not less than 64 per cent of the Third Plan outlay for Telangana.[25]

---

25. The Third Plan outlay for Telangana was Rs. 146.60 crore. See Government of Andhra Pradesh, "Facts about Telangana".

Appendix#

The following regression equations have been estimated:

(i)   Grants-in-Aid to States:

(1) $X_1 = 680.40 + 9.96^* X_2$ $R^2 = 0.41$ $N = 13$
        (3.61)

(2) $X_3 = 4.17 - 0.002\ X_5$ $R^2 = 0.004$ $N = 13$
        (0.007)

(3) $X_3 = 3.25 + 0.023\ X_4$ $R^2 = 0.003$ $N = 13$
        (0.128)

(4) $X_4 = 4.77 + 0.040^* X_5$ $R^2 = 0.49$ $N = 13$
        (0.012)

Where $X_1 =$ Grants-in-aid (Rs. in lakhs: average of 1957-58, 1958-59, 1959-60 and 1960-61)

$X_2 =$ Population of the state in millions (1961)

$X_3 =$ Grants-in-aid in rupees per capita (average of four years)

$X_4 =$ Own revenues in rupees per capita (average of four years)

$X_5 =$ Per capita income in rupees (1960-61)

Elasticity of own resources with respect to per capita income

$$= b. \frac{\overline{X_5}}{\overline{X_4}} = .04. \frac{328.2}{18.1} = 0.73$$

(ii) Central Assistance to States for the Third Plan:

(1) $X_1 = 73.81 - 0.30\ X_2$ $R^2 = 0.10$ $N = 14$
        (0.25)

(2) $X_1 = 84.46 - 0.067^{**} X_3$ $R^2 = 0.15$ $N = 14$
        (0.047)

(3) $X_2 = -7.22 + 0.14^* X_3$ $R^2 = 0.55$ $N = 14$
        (0.037)

(4) $X_1 = 84.79 - 0.079X_2 - 0.059X_3$ $R^2 = 0.155$ $N = 14$
        (0.391) (0.074)

(5) $X_4 = 68.36 + 3.79^* X_5$ $R^2 = 0.86$ $N = 14$
        (0.44)

Where $X_1 =$ Per capita Central assistance (in Rs.) for the Third Plan.

$X_2 =$ Per capita state contribution (in Rs.) for the Third Plan.

$X_3 =$ Per capita state income (in Rs.) in 1960-61.

$X_4 =$ Central assistance (Rs. in crore) for the Third Plan.

$X_5 =$ Population of the state (millions) in 1961.

Elasticity of state's own contribution with respect to per capita income

$$= b. \frac{\overline{X_3}}{\overline{X_2}} = 0.141. \frac{335.6}{40.1} = 1.18$$

Elasticity of Central assistance with respect to per capita income

$$= b. \frac{\overline{X_3}}{\overline{X_1}} = 0.067. \frac{335.6}{61.9} = 0.36$$

Note: * Significant at 5 per cent level.

** Significant at 20 per cent level.

\# Y. Satyanarayana assisted me in preparing this Appendix.

Economic and Political Weekly, October 18, 1969.

Sectoral Planning for Telangana

Some Issues for Consideration

A major task of Regional Planning for Telangana is the allocation of investment between the different sectors e.g., irrigation, power, communications, agriculture, industry, education and the programmes for weaker sections. For this purpose, it would be necessary to examine the sectoral allocations in the past with a view to ascertaining whether they were in keeping with the requirements of the region. Such an analysis would identify the sectors requiring special attention and would thus help to evolve the system of priorities and the strategies to be followed for the future. The data on the sectoral allocations in the past relate to the state as a whole and it is not possible from the data furnished so far to get a precise picture regarding such allocations for the Telangana region. There is, therefore, a need to explore the possibilities of compiling such information. The available data on irrigation, consumption of power, number of schools and scholars, road mileage etc., can be of some use for such an analysis.

Our Plans, whether at the state or Central level, have been concerned essentially with the development of infrastructure. However, the investment pattern at the state level (all states) is very much in favour of agriculture, irrigation and power whereas it is favourable to industry and communications at the Central level (see Table 8.1). Social services also account for a relatively larger proportion of investment at the state level as compared to the Centre. It may be noted that when compared to the experience of all the states, Andhra Pradesh has accorded a distinct priority for irrigation and power (about 53.7 per cent of total investment as against 40 per cent for all states). In the case of communications and social services, however, the allocations for Andhra Pradesh are significantly lower than for all states (22 per cent as against 33 per cent). The proportion allocated to communications and social services declined further to about

Table 8.1

*Statement Showing the Plan Outlays (in Crore) in the
First Three Plans in Andhra Pradesh, All States and All India*

Head of Development	Andhra Pradesh		All States (including Union Territory)		All India	
	Outlays	*Per cent*	*Outlays*	*Per cent*	*Outlays*	*Per cent*
	(1)	*(2)*	*(3)*	*(4)*	*(5)*	*(6)*
Agricultural Programmes, including Animal Husbandry, Fisheries, Cooperation and CD	128.32	20.12	1661.29	22.47	1942	12.72
Major and Medium Irrigation	172.32	27.02	1206.26	16.31	1521	9.97
Power	169.98	26.65	1753.89	23.72	1863	12.21
Industries and Mining	26.49	4.15	345.54	4.67	3177	20.81
Transport and Communications	29.95	4.70	633.80	8.57	3895	25.52
Social Services	110.74	17.36	1793.90	24.26	2865	18.77
Total	**637.80**	**100.00**	**7394.68**	**100.00**	**15263**	**100.00**

Source: Government of Andhra Pradesh, *Economic Development of Andhra Pradesh*, pp.74-75.

13 per cent during the subsequent three years whereas the allocation for power rose to 42 per cent (see Table 8.2) as against 27 per cent in the three plans. It would thus appear that Andhra Pradesh has considerably strengthened its infrastructure for agriculture through the provision of irrigation as well as the infrastructure for industry through investments in power. It is possible, however, that there has been some imbalance in the infrastructural investments for industry. This suspicion arises from the low and declining proportion allocated to transport and social services as also from a significant diversion of power to rural areas as indicated by the pace of rural electrification programme. Incidentally, the rural electrification programme does not seem to be tied up with the availability of ground-water, so that it is not possible to conclude that there is an optimum use of power provided for agriculture even if it is at the expense of industry.

Table 8.2

*Plan Outlays (in Crore) of Andhra Pradesh
during 1966-67, 1967-68 and 1968-69*

Head of Development	Outlays	Per cent
Agricultural Programmes	3634.04	15.34
Cooperation and CD	678.77	2.86
Irrigation	5622.48	23.73
Power	9936.90	41.93
Industry and Mining	662.10	2.79
Transport & Communication	738.76	3.12
Social Services	2401.15	10.13
Miscellaneous	24.30	0.10
Total	**23698.50**	**100.00**

Source: *Economic Development of Andhra Pradesh*, pp.153-154.

Irrigation

Although, as pointed out above, Andhra Pradesh has made substantial investments in irrigation, Telangana region has not received its due share in such investments. The growth of area under irrigation in the Telangana region was 15 per cent between 1956-57 and 1967-68 as against 18 per cent in the Andhra region, despite the fact that the proportion of cropped area irrigated is much lower in the Telangana region (see Table 8.3).[1] The use of electric power for irrigation in Telangana is also lagging behind the other regions. The number of oil engine pump sets per thousand acres of well-irrigated area in 1966-67 was 46 in Telangana as against 38.5 in the coastal region (see *Regional Development in Andhra Pradesh*, p. 12). On the other hand, the number of electric pump sets per thousand acres of well-irrigated area was 111 as against 145 in the coastal region (*Ibid.*, p.11). A better measure of the supply of power in relation to the needs is the number of electric pump sets per 1,000 acres of cropped area not served by canals and tanks, i.e., unirrigated area plus the area irrigated by wells. This

---

1. During 1996-1999, the percentage of not sown area irrigated in Telangana was 36, as against 40.7 for the state as a whole. In 1960-61, the proportion of irrigated area served by wells was 18.3 per cent in Telangana, which rose to 63.7 per cent by 1999-2000 (*Source:* S. Subrahmanyam (2003). "Regional Disparities: Courses and Remedies", in C.H. Hanumantha Rao and Mahendra Dev (edited), *Andhra Pradesh Development— Economic Reforms and Challenges Ahead*, Centre for Economic and Social Studies).

is because the ability to bring unirrigated area under well irrigation depends on the availability of cheaper sources of power. Measured thus, the disparity in the availability of power turns out to be much sharper. The number of electric pump sets per thousand acres of cropped area not irrigated by canals and tanks was 4.3 in Telangana in 1968-69 as against 7.2 in the coastal region (*Ibid.*, data on pp. 8, 10 & 11). These data indicate that private investment for irrigation on costly sources such as oil engines has been relatively more important in the Telangana region because of the insufficient benefits it has received from public investments on major and medium irrigation and rural electrification.

Table 8.3

Development of Irrigation in Andhra Pradesh

	Percentage of Irrigated Area to Cropped Area		Percentage Increase of Irrigated Area in
	1956-57	*1967-68*	*1967-68 over 1956-57*
Coastal Andhra	45.9	48.9	17.7
Rayalaseema	16.4	20.2	19.2
Andhra Region	33.0	37.3	18.1
Telangana	18.6	21.3	15.1
Andhra Pradesh	27.2	31.0	17.2

Source: Government of Andhra Pradesh, *Regional Development in Andhra Pradesh*, pp.7 & 8.

No comprehensive survey of groundwater resources has yet been made for Telangana. However, such of the information as is available seems to indicate that these resources may be meagre. For instance, the Techno-Economic Survey of Andhra Pradesh conducted by the National Council of Applied Economic Research (NCAER) states that, "the scope for large scale exploitation of ground water is absent (in Telangana) as the substrata are trap or granite, incapable of yielding prolific groundwater supplies" which explains why "about 12 per cent of wells in 1956-57 were not in use" (p.26). The Survey observes, however, that "Godavari river can very well be tapped in future to benefit the region, and the potential area for irrigation through the major and minor irrigation sources is estimated at 8.4 million acres". If such a potential exists and is economical to tap then it would represent at least a three-fold increase in the area irrigated at present.

It is obvious, however, that even if groundwater resources are meagre and available only in a few pockets, discovering such resources through geological survey and tapping them would have a high pay-off for a backward region like Telangana. Indeed, such a tapping is essential for a rational planning of rural electrification e.g., its regional allocation as well as phasing overtime. It would also be important to undertake a quick survey of tank irrigation with a view to determining to what extent and at what cost the present *ayacut* under tanks can be increased by renovating and improving the existing tank systems.

It is interesting to note that despite the slow progress of irrigation, the agricultural output (at current prices) increased at a higher rate (109 per cent) in Telangana than in Andhra region (91 per cent) between 1960-61 and 1966-67. The output of rice increased by as much as 102.5 per cent in Telangana as against only about 11 per cent in the Andhra region between 1956-57 and 1967-68 (see *Regional Development in Andhra Pradesh*, pp.4-5). This impressive performance may be attributable mainly to the substantial increase in fertilisers. The share of Telangana in the nitrogenous fertilisers distributed through government agency rose sharply from 12 per cent in 1957-58 to 27 per cent in 1967-68 with the result that consumption of such fertilisers per acre of gross irrigated area in Telangana reached the level obtaining in the Andhra region (*Ibid*, p.9). These facts about growth of agricultural output, especially of rice mainly through investments in fertilisers reinforce the earlier inference regarding the importance of private investments in the past as well as the possibility of impressive marginal returns from public investment in irrigation. However, as pointed out earlier, rural electrification to be effective for the purposes of irrigation, will have to be undertaken with an adequate knowledge of the availability of groundwater. Number of wells per thousand acres of cropped area as well as their depth can serve as a first approximation and villages can be ranked on this basis for the planning of rural electrification.

Power

As pointed out earlier, Andhra Pradesh has made substantial investments in power and a major portion of these investments during the Third Plan period was on thermal projects located in the Telangana region. It should be noted, however, that the per capita consumption of electricity in Telangana—both for industrial and agricultural purposes—is significantly less than in the Andhra region (see Table 8.4).[2] There is, therefore, considerable scope for stepping up power consumption in Telangana even from the available capacity, especially if the capital expenditure incurred on projects located in the region is to be debited to Telangana account as suggested by the Bhargava Committee in their Report on Telangana Surpluses.

Table 8.4

Per Capita Consumption of Electricity (kWh) in 1967-68

	Industrial	*Agricultural*	*Total*
Coastal Andhra	22.9	6.5	38.3
Rayalaseema	10.4	10.0	27.3
Andhra Region	19.0	7.6	34.9
Telangana Region	15.0	4.0	28.2
Andhra Pradesh	17.6	6.3	32.5

Source: *Regional Development in Andhra Pradesh*, p.17.

The future development of power in Telangana need not be rigidly limited by the demand originating in the region itself during the period of the perspective plan. In view of the need for the regional (consisting more than one state) and all-India grids for the optimum exploitation as well as utilisation of power resources in the country, it would be necessary to examine the comparative advantage of generating thermal power in the Telangana region. It may be noted in this context that Telangana has huge unexploited coal resources which, owing to their high ash content, are more suited to power generation than for coking purposes. Further, the unit costs of power generation from thermal plants decline significantly when the size of the plant is increased (see Government of India, *Report of Energy Survey of India Committee*, 1965: 136). However, it would be necessary to examine the comparative advantage of coal mining *vis-a-vis* the import of coking coal byproducts from washeries in other states (which are available virtually at zero cost) for power generation (see *Ibid.*, pp. 99-100). Given the costs of transportation from other regions, the cost of coal mining in the Telangana

---

2.   By 2001-02, per capita consumption of electricity in agriculture in Telangana was higher than in the rest of the state, due to its excessive dependence on well-irrigation.

region and its likely trend in future become relevant. Thus, apart from the existing cost levels, it would be interesting to know whether the prospects of coal mining in Telangana are in the nature of increasing returns (diminishing costs) or of diminishing returns (increasing costs).

If cost considerations are favourable, then the growth prospects for Telangana would be particularly bright. Coal mining being labour-intensive, would provide large employment opportunities and the availability of low-cost power can stimulate industrialisation by attracting capital and entrepreneurship from outside the region. The availability of large urban infrastructure as well as the uncertain prospects for agriculture in Telangana underline the need to explore the possibilities of power development.

Education

Secondary education shows by far the most impressive growth in Telangana in terms of number of schools as well as scholars whereas the growth has been lowest in the case of primary education (see Table 8.5) indicating a striking imbalance between the growth of primary and secondary education.[3]

Table 8.5

Number of Schools and Scholars in Telangana
(Percentage of Andhra Pradesh)

	Schools			Scholars		
	1956-57	1966-67	Per cent Increase	1956-57	1966-67	Per cent Increase
Primary	26.5	29.1	40.6	20.0	20.2	25.8
Middle	61.9	41.0	543.0	78.9	35.8	238.0
Higher Secondary	14.3	39.7	905.0	21.5	41.5	436.0
Colleges	30.6	42.6	166.7	23.8	38.9	206.5

Source: Government of Andhra Pradesh, *Regional Development in Andhra Pradesh*, pp. 21-23.

---

3. By 2001, the literacy rate in Telangana was 58.8 per cent as against 61.12 per cent for the state as a whole. In 2000-01, the drop-out rate for children in primary schools was 45.3 per cent in Telangana, as against 37.1 per cent in the state (*Source:* Subrahmanyam, 2003).

Since investment in secondary education is motivated by the job expectations or expected earnings, it reveals further an imbalance between investment in education and investment in material capital such as irrigation. Indeed, it is quite possible that both the low demand for primary education and greater demand for higher education arise from the low level of income in the region. Low income groups may not be in a position to send children to the primary schools mainly because they cannot afford to forego the earnings that the children bring for the family. On the other hand, the relatively well-to-do, who can afford secondary education may not find the traditional occupations, such as agriculture, attractive because of low and uncertain incomes. The higher demand for primary education in the Andhra region which accounts for 80 per cent of the primary students in the state (Table 8.5), may be explained, among other things, by the higher per capita income. Similarly, the lack of pressure for higher education in this region may be traceable to the existence of the relatively more attractive sources of earning. A district-wise analysis for the state shows a significant positive correlation between the per capita income from agriculture and the percentage of population attending the primary schools $(r = 0.46)$ or the percentage of children in the age group 0–11 attending primary schools $(r = 0.53)$. The data on the number of students, district-wise, are taken from the Statistical Abstract of Andhra Pradesh, 1969 and the data on the per capita crop output, district-wise, are taken from the Planning Department, Government of Andhra Pradesh.

The favourable impact of primary education on economic growth is well-known. Besides, expansion of primary education has a considerable exployment potential for those completing secondary education. A plan for compulsory primary education within the next decade or so would therefore be a good objective. This may involve the provision of mid-day meals for the children of the poor which can be met through a contribution or tax in kind on the rich farmers. The investments in the infrastructure for agriculture would raise its profitability and may thus lower the demand from farm children with land resources for jobs outside agriculture.

Weaker Sections

It is good to begin this section with the objectives and methods emphasised in the Fourth Plan in regard to the weaker sections of the society: "The basic goal is a rapid increase in the standard of living of the people, through measures which also promote equality and social justice ... there should be progressive reduction in the concentration of incomes, wealth and economic power and that benefits of development should accrue more and more to the relatively less privileged classes of society (p. 4).... In part these can be achieved by seeing that, in the implementation of programmes, the weakest are looked after first and the benefits of development are made to flow through planned investment in the underdeveloped regions and the more backward sections of the community (p. 28)." The above should serve to dispel the "growth first and equity next" notion which implies that measures for equity are mainly the concern of fiscal and other social policies. Growth itself should be achieved through measures which also promote equity. This is possible only if equity is made a major objective while planning investment itself. Secondly, equity should not be equated with the provision of some basic minimum to the poor through employment-oriented schemes which can be accomplished despite the increase in the inequalities in income and wealth.

Planning for the development of Telangana should, therefore, be much more than an exercise in aggregative magnitudes such as rates of growth, investment requirements and capital-output ratios, sectoral allocations etc. It should be concerned in a major way with the concrete programmes intended to serve the objectives of social justice and these should form an integral part of perspective plan for Telangana. In this context, the following programmes may be given a high priority in the formulation of the perspective plan for Telangana:

(a) Apart from the distribution of surplus lands (i.e., over and above ceilings), if any, to the landless, a comprehensive survey can be made of the culturable wastelands with the government and necessary investments made for their reclamation with a view to distributing them among the landless. Also, a fund can be created from public revenues for advancing loans to the small farmers, say of below 5 acres, for buying lands from the large landholders. Such a measure can tilt the land market in favour of the poor.

(b) Investment planning would be ineffective in achieving social objectives without credit planning. A credit plan especially for institutional credit in the agricultural sector should be prepared with a view to ensuring a specified portion of credit to the small farmers.

(c)   There seems to have been a significant progress towards the development of roads in Telangana. From 19 per cent of road mileage of the state in 1956-57, its share has risen to 30 per cent in 1965-66 (see *Regional Development of Andhra Pradesh*, p.19). However, there may be considerable scope for productivity raising rural works such as the renovation of tanks. In the choice of rural works, preference can be given to programmes which benefit the small farmers.

(d)   Programmes for the development of dairy and poultry industry on a small scale for the benefit of small and marginal farmers should be formulated. This industry offers a promising scope for augmenting the incomes of the poor, because the income elasticity of demand for such products is very high and the urban population is sizeable in Telangana. The demand for such products in the course of the next 15 to 20 years should be assessed and supplies planned with the necessary public investments to support the small units.

(e)   Educational planning should specifically provide for the promotion of education among the poor. Apart from the free mid-day meals to the poor children at the primary school level, this may involve a large number of freeships as well as free boarding facilities for the poorer sections.

Prepared as a Member of the Expert Group for the preparation of the Perspective Plan for Telangana, constituted by the Government of Andhra Pradesh.

Institute of Economic Growth, Delhi, July 31, 1971.

9

Statehood for Telangana
New Imperatives

In the recent by-election to the Lok Sabha from Karimnagar constituency, the voters were confronted with a choice between 'development' (within an integrated state) and 'separate Telangana'. The verdict went overwhelmingly in favour of 'separate Telangana'. By attributing this verdict to the 'sentiment' (for Telangana), some sections of the political leadership are evading the real issue. There was no religious or ethnic 'sentiment', not even of language, at issue in this election. One can, no doubt, read in this result, some assertion of 'regional identity', but this does not defy rational explanation. The simple and straightforward explanation is that the people perceive that 'development'—in the sense of equitable share in water resources, jobs, opportunities for enterprise and career advancement, and adequate voice in political decision-making—is not possible within the integrated state and that separate statehood alone can ensure justice for them.

The demand for separation is far more widespread now than in 1969 when the agitation for a separate Telangana was first launched. It has now engulfed farmers, youth and women on a much larger scale. The movement of the late sixties petered out not just because of the opportunism displayed by the leaders of the movement or due to the repressive measures of the state, as is often made out.

It was in the early seventies that Indira Gandhi's slogan of "Garibi Hatao" caught the imagination of the poor throughout the country. Her charisma continued in the South throughout the seventies. This was amply demonstrated when the Congress Party swept the polls in Andhra Pradesh in the late seventies even when Indira Gandhi lost power at the Centre. N.T. Rama Rao was another charismatic leader with a pro-poor and gender-sensitive agenda who won the widespread support of the poor in Andhra Pradesh in the eighties. The common people entertained high expectations from both the leaders and also trusted them in great measure because of the several anti-poverty programmes initiated by them. The credibility that they carried with the common people of Telangana was primarily responsible for sweeping the separatist movement under the carpet for quite some time.

However, the policies initiated by these charismatic leaders could not be sustained for long because of the absence of commitment and requisite political will among their successors. On the other hand, the period following the demise of these leaders witnessed a major shift in socio-economic policies. The neglect of agriculture, rural development and the social sectors in the post-liberalisation period, and the consequent rise in rural distress has brought into sharp focus the rise in regional disparities in development.

For example, in the 1980s, the per capita GSDP of the four richest states in the country was 100 per cent higher than that of the bottom four states, *viz.*, Bihar, Uttar Pradesh, Madhya Pradesh and Orissa. But by 1990s this disparity rose to 200 per cent. What is true of the rise in inter-state disparities in development would be true of regional disparities within some of the larger states, as the factors giving rise to such disparities are common.

A disquieting feature of the current political scene in Andhra Pradesh is that those still interested in the integrated state refuse to learn the right lessons from the developments since the first agitation for separate Telangana started. Otherwise, they would not have initiated a diversionary move like the constitution of the Second States Reorganisation Commission (SRC). Fifty years ago, the first SRC had recommended the formation of Telangana as a separate state in response to the simmering discontent in the region. The new SRC, in the present circumstances of widespread discontent, is most likely to endorse the recommendation of the first SRC.

If the motivation behind the constitution of the SRC is to avoid embarrassment from the people of the Andhra region in case Telangana is conceded immediately, and eventually to bring them round to the inevitability of separate statehood for Telangana, then the bargain may prove to be too costly, as this would open up a Pandora's box in terms of innumerable demands—just as well as unjust—for the constitution of separate states in the country. In any case, the move will fail to satisfy the people in Telangana, as they are no longer gullible, especially when the powers that be have refused to implement the recommendation of the first SRC.

Short of conceding separate statehood, a genuine and principled response to the present discontent in Telangana would be to embark upon a fresh round of land reforms and other socio-economic measures affecting the large majority of the disadvantaged sections; constitute regional planning and development boards consisting of elected representatives as well as experts; and make the whole planning process, including the sharing of resources transparent by making it accountable to the elected representatives. Further, the suggested special package for Telangana could be an additionality to the just share of Telangana in the existing resources. The execution of this package could be made an integral part of the regional planning process. However, even such a response may not carry much conviction in Telangana today, because it would be coming too late in the day and, in any case, the results from such experiments were disappointing in the past.

Over 80 per cent of the population in Telangana belongs to the disadvantaged social groups: SCs, STs and OBCs. Agrarian reforms were the prime agenda for the peasant movement in the 1940s. However, not enough time was available for this process of radical social transformation to run its course. In fact, it was interrupted with the integration of Telangana with the Andhra region, so that it still remains an unfinished task. In a larger and heterogeneous state like Andhra Pradesh, there is no adequate perception of this problem by the dominant political leadership that hails basically from the developed parts of the state.

Regional planning is not a new or uncharted course in Andhra Pradesh. This was tried earlier but soon abandoned for lack of earnestness and political will. And also because of the wrong notion that regional planning through elected representatives and the dissemination of relevant information would prove to be divisive by breeding regionalism. However, experience has clearly shown that shying away from regional planning through representative institutions and withholding information would produce the opposite result of intensifying the feelings of injustice and generating the demands for separation.

The SRC noted, more than 50 years ago, the fears of Telangana and anticipated the adverse social consequences if Andhra and Telangana regions are brought together to form an integrated state. The SRC emphasised that, within a time period of five years, two important issues needed to be sorted out: developing infrastructure in Telangana so as to bring it on a par with other regions; and preparing the people of Telangana for integration with Andhra through consensus. The SRC clearly stated that a merger should take place only if by two-thirds majority the legislators from the Telangana region agree to such a move. But, in practice, consensus among the people who do not belong to Telangana has been the guiding factor.

In pursuance of the Gentlemen's Agreement of 1956, the Telangana Regional Committee (TRC) was formed with elected representatives. The responsibility of this committee was to assess the available resources and allocate them to ensure proper development of the region. But in 1973 the TRC was abolished under the Six-Point Formula and the regional planning and development committees were constituted which, unlike the TRC, were not accountable to the elected representatives. However, these committees too have been abolished. There is virtually no mechanism now for regional planning and development.

But is development through regional planning and development committees and participatory institutions workable in a larger state composed of heterogeneous regions? Experience with politics of planning at the state level has shown that such a mechanism is not workable. Therefore, it can legitimately be argued that the political commitment necessary for a focused attention on the problems of growth and equity can be ensured only in the smaller states which are relatively homogeneous.

Take the case of Uttarakhand. The annual growth rate of its GSDP accelerated and reached the double-digit level in six years since it was formed.

It is perhaps too much to expect the requisite foresight and statesmanship from the dominant political leaders in Andhra Pradesh, who, in fact, have a track record of overpowering the central leadership, including even a towering personality like Pandit Jawaharlal Nehru, on the issue of separate statehood for Telangana.

But Nehru's vision and the prophecy of the SRC are knocking at our door again. One hopes that the present national leadership would positively and wisely respond to this call by initiating steps for the formation of separate Telangana state.

There would not be any significant resistance to the bifurcation of the state, as, even the people in the Andhra region are, by and large, reconciled to the inevitability of two Telugu speaking states. Most people would like to see an end to the current uncertainty.

The formation of separate Telangana would unleash the creative energies of the people by triggering off social transformation in the region. This would ensure social justice by bringing the weaker sections into positions of power and would improve governance both because of smallness of the state and better participation of the people.

The Hindu, January 8, 2007.

10 Regional Disparities, Smaller States and Statehood for Telangana

An Overview

Growing Regional Disparities in Development

Regional disparities in development have been growing in India, especially in the post-reform period. For example, according to the Eleventh Plan, the per capita GSDP of Bihar—the poorest state in the country—which had steadily declined to a little over 30 per cent of the per capita GSDP of the richest state by 1993-94, dropped further to 20 per cent in 2004-05 (GoI, 2008). What is true of rising inter-state disparities in development would be true of regional disparities within some of the larger states, as the factors contributing to such disparities would be the same in both the situations. The neglect of agriculture, rural development and the social sectors in the post-reform period, and the consequent rise in rural distress together with the concentration of private investment and proliferation of economic opportunities in the developed regions has brought into sharp focus the regional divide or the rise in inter-state as well as intra-state disparities in development.

Public investments in physical and social infrastructure have an equalising impact because they can be focused on backward regions. Further, public investment, in turn, induces private investment. But public investment has been falling over a period of time in the country. Public capital formation shrunk to 5 per cent of the GDP in the recent period from 10 per cent of GDP in the early nineties (Rao, 2006). According to the Eleventh Plan, over the past several years, the share of public investment in the overall investment has been declining reaching a little over 20 per cent in recent years. Therefore, according to the Planning Commission, there is "a very great limitation on the influence that fiscal quantities, allocations and strategy can directly exert on growth rates, especially at state level. States have, therefore, to focus on providing the necessary policy framework and supporting environment that makes economic activity possible and attractive enough for private sector investments" (GoI, 2008).

But can such a policy framework be effective in larger states for bringing in adequate investments and other benefits to the backward regions? The role of the state has changed dramatically from that of the main provider of investment in infrastructure in the pre-liberalisation period to a facilitator of private investment in the post-liberalisation period. The earlier role had a moderating influence on regional disparities insofar as backward regions also benefited to some extent from investments in infrastructure, whereas the new role is fraught with adverse consequences for these regions within larger states. This is because private investment and technology flow basically to the regions where physical and social infrastructure is already well-developed. In Maharashtra, for example, which has been among the top few states attracting private investments on a large scale in the post-reform period, the developed Pune-Nasik belt has received disproportionately large investments when compared to the backward Vidarbha and Marathwada regions.

Smaller States: Potential for High Growth

It is generally believed that economic liberalisation increases the role of the market while reducing the role of the state in economic activity. This is only superficially true. The relative roles of the market and the state do change in respect of the direct allocation of resources. But the impact of the state policies on the economy may turn out to be even greater if its role in influencing private sector investments is taken into account. The role of the government in awarding contracts, choice of locations for private sector projects and technical institutions, decisions about the number, type and location of special economic zones, land acquisition and compensation policies, various kinds of patronage extended to different enterprises and activities, etc., could together make a greater impact on the economy than in the pre-liberalisation period.

Indeed, this is the unmistakable impression one gets in the post-reform period in India, especially at the state level. In general, the impact seems to be in the direction of increasing inequalities between different regions and income groups, as is borne out by the official statistics on changes in private consumer expenditure and growth rates in GSDP. This is basically because official patronage in bigger states tends to favour the regions and income groups already endowed with adequate resources, skills, power and influence. This clearly shows that backward regions run the risk of losing the race to bigger states in the post-liberalisation era. At the same time, it shows that certain backward regions which can be constituted as viable states may use this enormous potential offered by state power effectively for their development.

This is borne out by the recent experience with the creation of smaller states like Chhattisgarh, Jharkhand and Uttarakhand. Their experience has been extremely encouraging in respect of the growth in GSDP. The Eleventh Plan document, lately approved by the National Development Council, gives the following telling figures showing that these states achieved growth rates far exceeding the targets set for the 10th Plan period, whereas the performance of their parent states, namely., Madhya Pradesh, Bihar and Uttar Pradesh fell considerably short of the targets (GoI, 2008):

State	*Targeted Growth Rate*	*Achieved (per cent per annum)*
Chhattisgarh	6.1	9.2
Madhya Pradesh	7.0	4.3
Jharkhand	6.9	11.1
Bihar	6.2	4.7
Uttarakhand	6.8	8.8
Uttar Pradesh	7.6	4.6

These high growth rates in GSDP lend credence to the proposition that the growth potential of these backward areas remained suppressed for long and their constitution into new states has released the creative energies of the people. Better governance may have also contributed to attracting private investment from outside as well as to better planning and utilisation of resources. This experience shows that the political commitment necessary for a focused attention on the problems of growth and equity can be better ensured in smaller states which are relatively homogeneous.

Development of Telangana

What is at issue is not whether development has been taking place. Indeed, in a democratic polity like ours some development has to take place in different parts of the country including even the remotest areas. The issue really is about the rate and quality or pattern of development. Apart from equity, such as due share in investment allocations, quality also refers to the cost, risks and sustainability of development.

There is a long-standing feeling that Telangana has not received its due share in investment allocations, and that the 'surpluses' from Telangana, i.e., the difference between what ought to have been spent and what has actually been spent, have been diverted to the other regions (Rao, 1969). For the Telangana region the per capita financial resources should be higher than the average for the Andhra Pradesh state, because, as for the Finance Commission transfer to states, 25 per cent of devolution is based on population and as much as 75 per cent is based on criteria like lower per capita income and other indicators of backwardness. Planning Commission transfers too have a significant weightage to low per capita income.

But there is no way of ascertaining exactly how public expenditures, as a whole, are distributed between different regions in Andhra Pradesh. The relevant information is not being disseminated ever since the abolition of the Telangana Regional Committee in 1973, under the wrong notion that sharing of such information would breed regionalism.

The growth that has been taking place in Telangana may be characterised as high cost growth. For example, the irrigation map of the region has changed completely. Tank irrigation occupied an important place a few decades ago. But now, over 70 per cent of irrigation is through groundwater and deep tube wells in large parts of Telangana (Subrahmanyam, 2003). This means for a unit output growth there has to be much greater investment now. Moreover, we do not have any information on such vital aspects as the quantity of water to be supplied for Telangana on account of the proposed irrigation projects including from 'assured' sources.

Further, farming has become highly risky in Telangana. For a given failure of rainfall, the fluctuations in output are much greater now when compared to the earlier decades. There is much greater distress being reported from the rainfed regions dependent on groundwater for irrigation where the suicide rates for farmers are high. Telangana region accounts for as many as two-thirds of the total number of farmers' suicides reported in the state between 1998-2006 (Galab *et al.*, 2009). The water crisis has affected sustainability: Land left fallow in Telangana has increased from 25 per cent of cultivable land in the early 1970s to as much as 40 per cent by 1999-2000 (Subrahmanyam, 2003). Pollution from industrial projects in certain areas has aggravated the crisis.

The feeling of injustice is greater among the educated classes, i.e., students, teachers, NGOs and professionals in general. This is explained by increasing awareness leading to greater sensitivity to 'discrimination' among such classes in respect of employment and promotions or career prospects, especially because of the rising importance of the services sector at higher levels of development. It is not surprising, therefore, that the separatist movement has gathered momentum in the post-reform period when the opportunities for such classes have proliferated in the services sector and the role of the state in influencing development and regional equity has vastly increased. For the same reasons, it should not also come as a surprise that the separatist sentiments are stronger in the relatively developed areas like North Telangana. Therefore, it can be concluded that far from 'development' programmes—more precisely, welfare measures currently being implemented—countering separatist sentiments, the movement for separation may become stronger with the spread of development as long as the perception of injustices due to 'discrimination' in development within the integrated state persists.

Socially Inclusive Telangana

Statehood for Telangana is a national issue and not just a regional one. This is because it represents the ongoing social change in the country for the empowerment of people through decentralised governance by broadening and deepening the working of our democratic system. Such empowerment and governance would enable articulation of the real problems of the people and their solution. This would inevitably result in *samajik* or 'socially inclusive' Telangana.

Inclusiveness could not be achieved so far in a bigger state because the voice of the disadvantaged sections remained fragmented. Experience shows that the entrenched interests are perpetuated in bigger and heterogeneous states because of their easy connectivity arising from their access to large resources, power and influence. The weaker sections, on the other hand, can come together, organise themselves and raise their voice effectively in a relatively homogeneous state because of common history and traditions and hence easy communicability.

For illustration, tribals are the most disadvantaged section socially and economically with negligible political voice. They live in remote areas and are subjected to land alienation on a large scale. Hardly any initiative has been taken so far in Andhra Pradesh to restore their lands despite the strong recommendations made by a high-level committee headed by a minister constituted by the present government (Government of Andhra Pradesh, 2006; Rao, 2007). There, the administration is alienated from the people and has been a breeding ground for extremist activities. But this has been treated not as a socio-economic issue, but mainly as a law and order problem. Because of this, the plight of the Girijans has been perpetuated and the extremist activities have been surfacing time and again, notwithstanding the claims of success in this regard by the authorities.

According to the 2001 Census, the ST population constitutes around 9 per cent in Telangana as against 5 per cent in the rest of the state. Thus, as much as 60 per cent of the ST population of Andhra Pradesh state is concentrated in Telangana. Their voice can be expected to be more effective in separate Telangana, not the least because their representation in the state legislature and other elected bodies would be proportionately greater.

Similarly, the population of Muslims is as high as 12.5 per cent in Telangana when compared to 6.9 per cent in the rest of Andhra Pradesh state. As many as 61 per cent of Muslims of Andhra Pradesh live in Telangana, of whom 60 per cent are spread over in different districts other than Hyderabad. They too can be expected to have greater political clout in separate Telangana in determining their fortunes as they can more easily relate themselves with the rest of the disadvantaged sections of the society in the struggle for a better and more secure livelihood. It must be noted in this context that social harmony between people professing different religions and speaking different languages has been proverbial in Telangana because of their shared history and traditions spanning over centuries.

The SCs account for about 16 per cent of population in Telangana as well as in the rest of AP. The census does not give the figures of OBCs. But we know from different sources that socially and economically disadvantaged sections, including SCs, STs and OBCs, constitute not less than 85 per cent of the population in Telangana.

Thus, the weaker sections constituting a large majority of population in Telangana and, for that matter, in Andhra would be better able to articulate their problems and politically assert themselves in separate, smaller and relatively homogeneous states. The formation of a Telangana state would thus strengthen the forces of social inclusion and secularism in both the states.

Inclusive Governance Feasible in Smaller States

The population of Telangana is over three-and-a-half crore now—much more than three crore for the whole of Andhra Pradesh at the time of its formation. The demands on governance have multiplied over this half a century. Apart from commitment to the development of the region, a smaller state being more easily accessible to the common people can intelligently and speedily grapple with their problems. Moreover, governance at the grassroots can be improved in a smaller state by strengthening the Panchayati Raj institutions which have been deprived of their functions, finances and functionaries. It is indeed ironical that the ruling party in Andhra Pradesh, which owes allegiance to Rajiv Gandhi, who visualised the 73rd and 74th Amendments to the Constitution, has not taken any initiative to revitalise these institutions. On the contrary, every attempt has been made to undermine these institutions by floating several top-down schemes and parallel implementation structures, even naming some of these schemes after Rajiv Gandhi! In smaller and relatively homogeneous states like Telangana and Andhra, the empowerment of these local elected institutions can be expected to be high on the agenda, among other things, because of the greater pressures these elected representatives can bring to bear on the new establishments.

Consensus for Telangana

The committee headed by Pranab Mukherjee is supposed to be engaged in due consultations for ascertaining whether there is consensus for Telangana state. But the Congress Party's own position on Telangana is not made clear to this committee. Even if the second SRC were to be constituted, as per the Congress Election Manifesto of 2004, the party could not possibly have remained non-committal on the issue, as most of the parties would have made their position clear to the SRC.

If the Congress supported statehood for Telangana, there would have been a majority in Parliament in favour of such a Bill. But, if the Bill could not have been introduced because of lack of consensus in the United Progressive Alliance, or the government running the risk of losing power, then people would have understood the constraints, provided the Congress' own position was made clear. Spelling out its position as a party did not, by itself, pose any risk to the government.

The real explanation for the Congress not taking a stand is the 'veto power' being exercised by a few leaders in power in the state, which in fact is the genesis of the formation of Andhra Pradesh. This demonstrates how a few individuals representing numerically small social groups can manipulate the levers of power in a large and heterogeneous state by dint of the huge resources and power at their command. Yet, they have been telling the people, time and again, that they will abide by the decision of their 'High Command'. But the fact of the matter is that these individuals are able to mislead and overpower their 'High Command' by dint of their resources and numbers in Parliament.

All the major political parties in Andhra Pradesh, except the Congress and the CPM, have unequivocally come out in favour of the formation of a separate Telangana state. Even within the Congress party, there is a concensus in its favour among the leaders, legislators, ministers in the state as well as the Centre belonging to Telangana.

The demand for Telangana state is not opposed by the common people from the rest of the state of Andhra Pradesh, notwithstanding hostility from certain sections of business and political elite. This is amply borne out by the stand taken in favour of separate Telangana state by parties like the Telugu Desam headed by Chandrababu Naidu, CPI, BJP, Praja Rajyam Party headed by Chiranjeevi and others.

But then what does one mean by consensus? The first States Reorganisation Commission (SRC), which recommended in 1956 formation of the separate Hyderabad state consisting of Telangana, defined consensus as the one reached among the Telangana people themselves. This is clear from its recommendation that after five years, Telangana could be merged with Andhra only if two-thirds of the Telangana legislators opted for it. But consensus now has come to mean among every one at the national and state levels, except the people of Telangana!

This is not quite fair because, in the first place, Telangana was merged with the Andhra region in 1956 without ascertaining the wishes of the people of Telangana through their elected representatives as recommended by the SRC. Secondly, when there is a clear opposition to statehood for Telangana from sections of the power elite belonging to the dominant region of the state, it is not fair to insist upon consensus among all the constituent regions when the issue concerns a particular region only. Pandit Jawaharlal Nehru, the then Prime Minister, had openly stated that there should be a divorce between Andhra and Telangana, if the latter so desired at any future date.

The demand for the second SRC to settle the issue could have some basis if the first SRC recommended the formation of composite Andhra Pradesh state, and disrupting such an arrangement, it could be argued, would require re-examination of the whole issue by a similar high level expert and quasi-judicial body. But the first SRC had recommended the formation of Telangana state after examining all the relevant aspects and their recommendation was not honoured.

In a situation like this, the will of the people of Telangana, as expressed by the large majority of the legislators from the region, can alone be the guiding principle. This has been expressed time and again in favour of separate statehood in the last four decades through the democratic process vindicating the position taken by the SRC. Even in the by-elections held in May 2008, it is common knowledge that the major political parties, including the Congress, approached the voters pledging themselves in favour of statehood for Telangana. Therefore, in the case of this last election, the rallying slogan of different parties favouring Telangana should be taken as an index of support for separate statehood.

Despite this background, the recent decision of the state government on the last day of the final session of the State Assembly to constitute a committee, consisting of the representatives of both the State Assembly and the Legislative Council, for examining the issues connected with statehood for Telangana will not carry any credibility whatsoever. This has only strengthened the suspicion that it is a diversionary move on the eve of the general elections, especially in the light of the past experience that even the recommendation made by a high level body like the SRC favouring Telangana was ignored by the powers-that-be. This move is virtually a non-starter as major political parties have declined to nominate their representatives on this committee.

Broadbased, Non-Partisan Movement

Leaders from Telangana have been going to Delhi for making representations in most rational terms; they have even been called to Delhi occasionally by the 'High Command' but basically, it is the power structure in Andhra Pradesh that has become decisive in determining the outcomes. Therefore, the focus of action for achieving separate Telangana has not been Delhi alone; it has been backed by the peaceful and democratic movement in villages and towns in the Telangana region.

Political parties espousing separate Telangana have been engaged in electoral battles. This is understandable because the decision to carve out a separate state is ultimately a political one involving Parliament and governments at the Centre as well as the state. But the movement for separate Telangana itself has not been 'engineered' by political parties as some people would have others believe. Rather, the political parties supporting separation have been receiving sustenance from the deep-seated and widespread sentiment for separate statehood for Telangana nurtured by various movements—political as well as non-political, including the *Mulki* agitation—since the times much before the formation of Andhra Pradesh.

It is, however, true that some political parties have displayed opportunism by building up their political fortunes using this sentiment and betraying the cause once their narrow purpose was fulfilled. But despite such betrayals, the broad political movement for separate statehood itself has survived and gained strength, beyond electoral considerations, because of its genuineness and deep-seated social base.

Such an independent movement has been complementary to electoral politics and served to ensure the accountability of the elected representatives.

The experience of Uttarakhand has been instructive in this respect. After getting disgusted over repeated betrayals by the political parties, the intelligentsia there took charge of a broadbased, non-partisan movement, led and nurtured it by educating and building awareness among the people at large, and ultimately succeeded in achieving separate statehood.

References

Galab, S., E. Revathi and Prudhvikar Reddy (2009). "Farmers' Suicides and Unfolding Agrarian Crisis in Andhra Pradesh", in D. Narasimha Reddy and Srijit Mishra (ed.), *Agrarian Crisis in India*. New Delhi: Oxford University Press.

Government of India, Planning Commission (2008). *Eleventh Five Year Plan (2007-2012)* Vols. I&III. New Delhi.

Government of Andhra Pradesh (2006). *Report of the Land Committee*.

Rao, C.H.H. (1969). "Budgetary Surpluses of Telangana", *Economic and Political Weekly*, October 18.

———. (2006). "Growing Regional Disparities in Development in India—Post-Reform Experience and Challenges Ahead", Lecture dedicated to the Memory of Professor A.M. Khusro, delivered at the 88th Annual Conference of the Indian Economic Association, held at Visakhapatnam, 27-29 December, 2005; published in *The Indian Economic Journal*, 54(I), April-June.

———. (2007). "Land Reforms in Andhra Pradesh", *The Hindu*, September 13.

Subrahmanyam, S. (2003). "Regional Disparities: Causes and Remedies", in C.H.H. Rao and Mahendra Dev (ed.), *Andhra Pradesh Development—Economic Reforms and Challenges Ahead*.

This article is based on the Seventh Prof. B. Janardhan Rao Memorial Lecture delivered at the Kakatiya University, Warangal, February 27, 2009. See *Mainstream*, March 7, 2009.

Epilogue

At the time of this writing (January 18, 2010), the agitations for separate statehood for Telangana in the Telangana region as well as for Samaikhya (United) Andhra Pradesh in the Andhra region are in full swing. The agitation in Telangana is unprecedented in its sweep, being universal or, at any rate, far more widespread than in 1969, involving, among others, students, farmers, women and even children. The movement is virtually taken over and led by the students, all of whom were obviously born at least a decade after the agitation of 1969. It appears as if history is repeating itself or time is standing still for over four decades so far as this issue is concerned!

Curiously, in the case of the Andhra region, history appears to have been overturned. The 'Jai Andhra' or separate Andhra agitation of 1972-73 was triggered-off by the land reform legislation and the validation of Mulki Rules (preference for natives of Telangana in employment) by the Supreme Court, because of which the big landed sections as well as educated youth could lose in the integrated state. Over the last four decades, however, certain leading business sections including those involved in real estate business from the Andhra region developed a big stake in Telangana, particularly in and around Hyderabad city. Thanks to the lopsided urbanisation and concentration of financial sector services and IT industry in Hyderabad in the post-reform period, the educated youth—most of whom born after the 'Jai Andhra' agitation like their Telangana counterparts—could understandably have developed an emotional identification with the capital city and so a stake in Samaikhya (United) Andhra Pradesh.

Guided by the consensus among the major political parties in favour of the formation of separate Telangana state, as espoused in their election manifestos and reiterated by them as recently as 7th December 2009, the Central government on 9th December announced its decision to initiate the process for the formation of Telangana state. Within hours, this decision triggered off a counter-agitation in the Andhra region for united Andhra Pradesh, leaders of the major political parties taking sides by getting divided horizontally on regional lines. It is not clear whether the leaders did not mean what they promised all these years on Telangana in the expectation that no worthwhile initiative would come from the Centre or could not anticipate the public reaction in the event of any favourable move on the issue. In any case, this has placed the Centre in a difficult situation leading to the stalemate in the resolution of the crisis.

As it is, the Constitution fully empowers the Centre to carve out new states, the role of the state legislatures being limited to merely expressing their views on the proposed Bill by the Centre. While politics cannot be wished away in a democracy and the Centre cannot normally be expected to proceed against the wishes of the majority of legislators of a state, ultimately, politics in a democracy have to come to terms with the provisions of the Constitution and respect the universal demand of the people of a region for a separate statehood. Also, in the long run, the youth of any region in the modern age, imbued as it would be with the democratic spirit, would come to respect peoples' wishes from the other region for separate statehood. Besides, a pride in the capacity to develop opportunities in one's own state is bound to come into play. Addressing the legitimate concerns of the stakeholders is essential to facilitate this process.

There is no alternative to the Centre as well as the leaders of both the regions taking initiatives for a constructive dialogue for resolving the outstanding issues by addressing the legitimate concerns of the stakeholders, to pave the way for separate statehood for Telangana and thus end the perpetual uncertainty undermining the harmonious development of both the regions. While agitations are necessary for the assertion of legitimate rights, in a democracy, constructive dialogue is indispensable for bringing such aspirations to fruition.

Appendices

Appendix I

*A Note on the Movement for Separate Telangana** *

I am one of those who had actively participated in the movement for Vishal Andhra in 1955. Observing the movement for Separate Telangana now as an outsider, I am particularly struck by the political awakening of the people—the consciousness of their rights and the capacity to organise themselves as well as the readiness to make heavy sacrifices for the attainment of their goal. There is a decisive shift from a phase a decade ago when even a moderate movement required a strong and highly motivated leadership to the present one when the people themselves have spontaneously launched a movement with a strong will and organising ability and are winning over the political leadership to their side. The movement for Separate Telangana is thus unprecedented in many respects. All this has been made possible owing to the successful practice of democracy during the last 20 years, which has immensely contributed to the political awakening of the people.

Moreover, a large organised and vocal class has emerged in Telangana, in the course of the last decade and a half of socio-economic development, comprising NGOs, students, teachers, engineers, etc. These sections strongly feel that their interests can be protected only in a separate state. Experience has convinced them that even in a democracy it would be difficult to ensure economic justice to a minority region so long as political power is exercised by the majority region. It is clear to any observer that if the Central government refuses to concede separate Telangana state now, it will have to bow down to the wishes of the people after the general elections in 1972.

But is separation desirable in the larger interests of Telangana? From a purely political angle, since a strong sense of regional identity persists among the people of Telangana, separation may promote a sense of responsibility and ensure greater effort for the development of the region. The denial of the opportunity for the independent management of their affairs may breed persecution complex thus

---

* Written in 1969.

undermining the sense of individual dignity and interregional solidarity without which no genuine socio-economic development would be possible.

There is no reason to doubt the economic viability of separate Telangana state. The States Reorganisation Commission had clearly pointed out that Telangana would have revenue surplus as against the deficit in Andhra. Owing to the historical factors the per capita tax revenue in Telangana has been much higher than in Andhra. In view of the undisputed fact that large amounts of Telangana surpluses have been diverted to the Andhra region, it is clear that separation would enable Telangana to step up its investment whereas Andhra may face serious budgetary deficits. But Andhra can get over its deficits by scrapping prohibition and by increasing the tax effort.

As to the growth prospects of separate Telangana state, it is necessary to bear in mind the two basic factors which have become decisive for economic growth: the increasing role of government or public sector investment and the increasing significance of education and skills (or human capital) in economic growth. The role of public sector investment has been increasing everywhere in the world irrespective of the ideologies to which the government subscribe. In India, the share of public sector investments in the total national investment has risen to over 50 per cent. Therefore, the rate of economic development of a region depends very much on its share in public investments. Experience has shown that it would be difficult for Telangana to get its due share in government outlays in an integrated state.

Secondly, the economic growth of a region is no longer adequately measured by the material capital—buildings, roads, factory structures etc. It will be dependent crucially on the human capital of the region, *viz.*, the education and technical skills embodied in the people inhabiting the region. The growth experience of many countries of the world in the recent period has shown that human capital contributed as much as 50 per cent to the increase in per capita income. Experience in Telangana has shown that it is far more difficult to ensure an adequate share in human capital than in material capital. The discrimination against the Telangana personnel in regard to the training, employment and promotion at various levels has resulted in less than adequate share in human capital. There is thus every reason to believe that separation would create conditions for the proper development of material as well as human resources of the region. Therefore, creation of separate Telangana appears not only politically inevitable but also desirable for the speedy development of the region.

Appendix II

*Letters to the Editor**
National Herald, July 20, 1969

Telangana

Sir—I am one of those who had actively participated in the movement for the formation of the present state of Andhra Pradesh in 1955. I have had an opportunity to observe the agitation for a separate Telangana during this summer as an outsider. There was a time when even a moderate political movement required a strong and highly motivated leadership. But the present agitation is unprecedented. The people themselves have spontaneously launched it.

Any person visiting Telangana now after a decade and a half would be struck by the emergence of a large organised and vocal class comprising NGOs, students, teachers, engineers, lawyers, physicians, businessmen, etc. These sections strongly feel that their interests can be protected only in a separate state. They narrate how experience has convinced them that it would be difficult to ensure economic justice to Telangana, so long as political power is exercised by the Andhra region. The feeling for separation is so intense and widespread that in all probability the Union government will have to bow down to the wishes of the people, at any rate, after the general elections in 1972.

To understand the tensions brewing in Telangana, it is necessary to bear in mind the increasing role of Government or public investments and the crucial significance of education and skills in economic growth. Telangana failed to get even one-third of the Government outlays in the integrated state, despite the fact that Telangana accounts for 35 per cent of the population of the state and its per capita tax revenue is higher and per capita income lower than in Andhra. In view of the widely accepted fact that the revenue surpluses of Telangana have been diverted to the Andhra region, a general feeling persists that separation would enable Telangana to step up its investment. The discrimination against the Telangana personnel in regard to the training, employment and promotion at various levels has demonstrated that it is far more difficult to ensure an adequate share in education and skills than in public outlays.

In these circumstances, it would appear that separation alone can ensure greater effort from the people of Telangana for the development of the region. The denial of the opportunity for the independent management of their affairs may

---

* This letter to the editor was carried in other major national dailies, including *The Statesman* (July 15, 1969), *The Times of India* (July 15, 1969).

breed persecution complex, thus undermining interregional solidarity without which no genuine socio-economic progress would be possible.

Those who decry the idea of a separate Telangana in the name of national integration ignore that this agitation is motivated by the desire to ensure an equitable share in the fruits of socio-economic growth. The Telangana agitators include, apart from the Telugu-speaking people of the region, those speaking Urdu, Hindi, Marathi, Kannada, Tamil, Gujarati and several other Indian languages. Even those of the Andhra region who settled down in Telangana before the formation of Andhra Pradesh are active in this agitation. Thus, for the first time in the recent period, one finds rational economic considerations deminating over those of language, religion and caste. Therefore, the sooner our leaders grasp the nature of the emerging forces, the better it would be for the balanced growth of the country on secular and democratic lines.

C.H. Hanumantha Rao
Institute of Economic Growth,
University Enclave,
Delhi - 7

Appendix III

*Letters to the Editor**

Hindustan Times, January 30, 1973

Sir—It is unfortunate that the national leadership has become insensitive to genuinely broad-based movements. Unanimous resolutions passed by widely attended conventions fall to impress our leaders. Hence, the incentive for violent expression of discontent.

There seems to be no point blaming the so-called vested interests for the present situation in the Andhra region. If the ruling party was really capable of implementing radical measures such as land reforms and development programmes designed to increase employment opportunities the separatist movement would not have gained such momentum at all. Because of the inherent limitations to the expansion of job opportunities, the only way of avoiding recurring regional tensions in Andhra Pradesh would be to bifurcate the State. The people will then be able to see the more lasting solutions and show more initiative, drive and confidence as they did in the case of Punjab and Haryana after the States were separated.

There are powerful vested interests at the Centre who are concerned not so much about the fate of the people in strife-torn Andhra Pradesh as about the consequences of its bifurcation for their own home states. Apparently they fear the loss of their position at the Centre if their home states become smaller. Another group at the Centre comprises those who have blocked the communication channels between the people and the leaders because their assessment of the Andhra situation as well as the suggested remedies are those that are likely to please the Prime Minister rather than those that conform to the realities in the state.

It is true that bifurcation might open up a series of issues such as the division of assets and liabilities, distribution of the waters of the Krishna-Godavari and the future of Rayalaseema and the location of the capital of the Andhra state. These could prove difficult to tackle and could well hold up progress in the two states if they are not sorted out in time. The leaders of the region have already volunteered to settle these. The Centre should ask them to examine these thoroughly and come to an agreed formula before it bifurcates the area.

C.H. Hanumantha Rao
Institute of Economic Growth,
University of Delhi,
January 24, 1973

---

* This letter written in response to the separate Andhra agitation was carried in other major national dailies.